Safe AND *Secure* in the Hands of JESUS

Safe AND Secure in the Hands of JESUS

David Boudreaux

Safe and Secure in the Hands of Jesus
© 2023 by David Boudreaux. All rights reserved.

No part of this publication may be reproduced, distributed, or transmitted in any form or by any means, including photocopying, recording, or other electronic or mechanical methods, without the prior written permission of the author, except in the case of brief quotations embodied in critical reviews and certain other noncommercial uses permitted by copyright law.

GENRE: SPIRITUALITY, RELIGION

Printed in the United States of America

ISBN 979-8-8689-8697-0 (paperback)
ISBN 979-8-8689-8698-7 (ebk)

2023 | 11 | 03

Table of Contents

DEDICATION 1
Chapter 1   My Testimony 3
Chapter 2   God's Plan 11
Chapter 3   Everlasting Life 20
Chapter 4   The Unpardonable Sin 27
Chapter 5   Salvation is a Free Gift from God 34
Chapter 6   Saved Sinners 42
Chapter 7   Salvation is a Relationship 47
Chapter 8   God's Omnipotence 53
Chapter 9   The Bride of Christ 63
Chapter 10 No Condemnation 70
Chapter 11 A Gift from the Father 77
Chapter 12 Perfect Love Casteth Out Fear 87
Chapter 13 The Holy Spirit 94
Chapter 14 The Rapture 104
Chapter 15 Great Joy in Heaven 113
Chapter 16 The Lamb of God 121
Chapter 17 Reservations in Heaven 129
Chapter 18 We are Children of Promise 138
Chapter 19 The Lambs Book of Life 146
Chapter 20 The Light of the World 150

Chapter 21 Predestination 160

Chapter 22 Ambassadors for Christ 170

Chapter 23 Led by the Spirit 179

Chapter 24 Born Again 191

Chapter 25 The Devil Will Cause Doubt 200

Chapter 26 What if I Fall? 210

Chapter 27 Purpose and Summary 214

DEDICATION

I want to thank the Lord first of all, for the guidance of the Holy Spirit during this entire process. It is still amazing to me how God gives me the words right when I need them. Sometimes those words come in the middle of the night, never-the-less, Praise the Lord. I first decided to tackle this project because there seems to be so much confusion and doubt concerning whether or not people are sure about their salvation. I don't believe there should be any question about that because if you have accepted Christ as your savior it should have changed your whole life. I think after someone reads this book they will know one hundred percent for sure if they are saved or not. Then, there are the questions concerning the security of our salvation. There are many religions that teach that our salvation is based on our behavior both before and after salvation. The fact is your salvation has nothing to do with your behavior either before or after you are saved and I'm going to show you why. After much prayer, dedication, devotion and study, I don't think there should be any question about the security of our salvation either. I think God wants us to know where we stand with Him and He has given us all the answers we need in

His Word. I am dedicating this work to my wonderful wife Mona D. Boudreaux for several reasons. First, because she knew that I had desired to write for a long time and just recently the Lord told me He wanted me to write for Him. I have been wondering how I could best serve the Lord for some time now. I asked her what she thought and she gave me an extensive amount of encouragement and support. Second, because this work took a lot of my time and dedication and she went out of her way to pick up the slack around the house to make it happen. Third, she is the one who inspired the writing of this book because this whole project began with me trying to answer some of her questions concerning the security of her salvation. That research led to the publishing of my first Spiritual book called "Heaven Bound". After the Book was published I was not satisfied that it answered all of the possible questions concerning this topic and I didn't feel that it met the standards that it should for God's work. This book is a rewrite of the first book I wrote on this topic. I just want to say thank you to my help mate and thank the Lord for leading her to me. I pray that this work will help many people answer questions they have concerning their salvation and the security of their salvation.

Your humble servant
David W. Boudreaux

CHAPTER ONE

My Testimony

Looking for God

If you have been searching for God, but you aren't sure how, or where, to find Him this book was written for you. If you have felt all of your life that there is an empty space deep inside of you, a longing, a desire, or a void that can never be filled and you are looking for answers, then this book is for you. If you are that person thinking that there has to be more to life than what I am experiencing, then this book is for you. If you have felt a constant tug on your heart from an unknown source and you just aren't sure how to respond, this book is for you. If you think you received Christ as your savior as a young child, but you have not lived a life for God and now you not sure about your salvation status, this book is for you. If you have had some sort of religious experience in your life, but you're not certain about what it meant, or what was expected of you afterwards, this book is for you. If you are not certain whether you are a child God or not, then this book is for you. If you were once saved by accepting Jesus Christ as your savior, but you no longer trust God, or you have denied Christ since then, this book is for you. If you have had loved ones who have passed into the next life and you're not sure where they are spending eternity, this book has the answers you seek. If you're not sure if a Christian can lose their salvation after they were saved, or not, and if they can, then is it possible to be saved again, this book is for you. If you believe that you will go to heaven some day because you are a good person, this book was written for you. If you are someone who believes in God and you think that this belief alone will save your soul, this book is for you. If you are a religious person who goes to church regularly and you believe that your church attendance will get you to heaven, this book is for you. I am a born again child of the Almighty Living God and I know 100% for sure that I am heaven bound and there is no power in heaven, on earth, or in hell that can change that. If you can't make that statement with absolute certainty and know in heart that it is true, this book is for you. I know that my salvation is safe and secure in the hands of God.

Good Works Cannot Save You

First of all, I will just start out by saying this, being a good person, or doing good works, cannot save your soul. Hell is a place that God created for the Devil and his angels. It is a place of torment for all eternity designed to punish Satan for his rebellion against the almighty creator of all things. (Matt 25:41) Believing that there is a god is not sufficient to save your soul. Being a religious person or someone who attends church on a regular basis does not save you. Being a good church member and dedicating your time to help others at your church will not save you. Having a religious experience such as speaking in tongues, or a miracle healing, or such like, does not make you a Christian. The good news is if you are searching for God, or looking for answers to these questions concerning your eternal destiny, or if you are wondering if you are saved or not, "GOD HAS A PLAN".

Going to Church Doesn't Save You

God's plan is for everyone on the face of the earth to have an opportunity to hear the gospel, (Gospel means good news) and to either make a conscious choice to accept it as the truth, or to reject it. The good news is that God has a plan for the salvation of your soul. I was raised in the Catholic Church. My family attended church regularly, not every time the doors were open, but at least every Sunday. (Unless my dad had a hunting or fishing trip planned for a certain weekend.) I attended Sunday school. I was baptized as an infant. I was an altar boy for a short time. I had my first communion and I was appointed God parents, **but, I was not saved!** I'm not suggesting here that Catholic folks in general are not saved; I'm just saying that I was religious, but I personally did not know God. Being religious, or going to church regularly, or trying to be a good person is not the path to salvation. Jesus told Nicodemus the religious leader, a Pharisee, that in order to enter into the kingdom of heaven you must be born again and until I was twenty five years old I had never heard that term and certainly had no idea what it meant.

> *"Jesus answered and said unto him, Verily, verily, I say unto thee, Except a man be born again, he cannot see the kingdom of God"*
> *(John 3:3)*

The Presentation of the Gospel

When I was twenty five I was in the United States Air Force stationed at Peterson Field Air Force base in Colorado Springs Colorado. While I was there I met a Christian family that I grew rather close to. One Easter Sunday they invited me to attend church with them. I was not too keen on going to church in those days, but they said all Christians should attend church at least on Easter Sunday. Thinking that I was a Christian at the time, and not wanting to appear otherwise, I reluctantly agreed to go. It just happened that during this Easter service they were going to do something different than usual. They were playing an audio tape of the re-enactment of the crucifixion of Christ. This was a very realistic audio tape. It had all the voices and all the sounds just like you were there watching it happen right in front of you. When the audio tape they were playing reached the part where they were driving the nails into Jesus' hands and feet, as they nailed Him to the cross, it felt like those spikes were being driven straight into my heart. I came under such deep conviction at that moment that I had to get up and leave the service. I did not understand at the time exactly what was happening to me, or even what I was feeling. I thought I was already a Christian at the time. I went outside and waited for the service to end. When my friends came out of the building and they asked where I went, I told them that I had to use the restroom. I wasn't fooling God though, and frankly I don't think I was fooling anyone else either.

The Conviction

Someone once told me I was the best Christian, non-Christian, they had ever met. At the time I didn't appreciate that statement because I thought I was a Christian and I didn't understand why they thought they were any better than I was. Truth be known, I had been searching for God for a long time even though I thought I knew Him already. I just didn't know what I was supposed to be feeling. I had tried to do the right thing and go to church occasionally and treat others well, but I was not a born again child of God and after that day I knew something wasn't quite right. That night I had what I thought was a very strange dream. I was walking downtown in Colorado Springs with my friends when all of a sudden there was a loud noise coming from the heavens. I'm not sure what the noise was, but a few seconds later I started seeing people rise up off the ground and float into the sky. One by one they rose up and disappeared into the clouds. My friends, whom I knew were Christians, also began to rise up and I was left standing there alone. There were other people who were left behind as well, but all the ones who were near to me were taken. I knew at that moment that I had been left behind because God had given me an opportunity to hear the gospel and even though I did not out-right reject it, I had been offered a chance to accept Christ and I had not done so. I woke up in a cold sweat, scared to death that I had missed my window to salvation. I began to search around in an effort to verify my suspicions that other people that I knew who were saved had been taken also. I had seen hundreds of people go up into the clouds and disappear in my dream and I was left. I had to make sure this hadn't really happened; thankfully it had not, at least not yet.

The Salvation Experience

The whole following week God continued to work on me. I had never experienced a dream so real and so vivid before and I could not stop thinking about it. I could remember every detail, especially how it made me feel being left behind. I felt so bad about having heard God's plan for salvation and not responding to it, that by the time the following Sunday came around I was fruit so ripe on the tree that if I had not been harvested, I would have fallen off the tree on my own. I anxiously went back to another church the next weekend. I knew there was going to be an invitation at the end of the service and all I could think about was, I wished this preacher would stop talking and skip straight to the invitation. Eventually he did stop talking and I was out in the isle headed to the front of the church before the organ player had a chance to strike the first note. At this point my need to be saved had become a matter of urgency, I was not about to take the chance of being left behind another week.

Later when I shared my dream with the pastor of the church where I had accepted Christ, he told me that God had given me a vision of the rapture. The rapture is what they call the time when Jesus comes back to take all born again Christians to their new home in heaven. (I Cor 15:51-52) I don't think I had ever heard the term rapture before that day, but God knew what I needed to see in order for me to do what I needed to do. Before this all happened I had lived a good life. I had been raised religiously. I had experienced a lot of the things that the world had to offer a young man. Yet, I knew that deep in my soul there was an empty hole that nothing this world had to offer could fill. Since that day I have never felt that emptiness again.

After I was saved, there developed in me such a great hunger for the Word of God that I could hardly put the Bible down except to go to the restroom or to work. I had a hunger for the Word of God like a new born child hungers for its mother's milk. What I had just experienced was a re-birth and as a new born Christian I was hungry for spiritual food. This comes from the Word of God. I have known ever since that day that God has plans for me and it was only a short time later when I answered His call for me to go to Bible College. The rest is history, but the point is that God had a plan for me and He has one for you as well. His plan begins with your redemption, the washing away of your sins, and the salvation of your soul.

Chapter Two

God's Plan

Are You Searching for God?

If you have had an empty place inside of you, if you have been searching for answers from God concerning your eternal destiny, then you need to understand that God has been working on you since the day of your birth to prepare you for what He has planned for you. To prepare you to hear the gospel and to be ready to accept the free gift of salvation that He has made available to you.

This is God's plan for your salvation:

The first step towards salvation from the destiny of eternal separation from God in a place called hell is to realize that you need to be saved. We need a savior because we are all sinners and fall short of the glory of God.

> *"As it is written, There is none righteous, no, not one:" (Rom 3:10)*
>
> *"They are all gone out of the way, they are together become unprofitable; there is none that doeth good, no, not one." (Rom 3:12)*
>
> *"Whose mouth is full of cursing and bitterness:" (Rom 3:14)*
>
> *"Now we know that what things soever the law saith, it saith to them who are under the law: that every mouth may be stopped, and all the world may become guilty before God." (Rom 3:19)*
>
> *"Therefore by the deeds of the law there shall no flesh be justified in his sight: for by the law is the knowledge of sin." (Rom 3:20)*
>
> *"For all have sinned, and come short of the glory of God;" (Rom 3:23)*

I'm a Good Person

You may think that you are a good person and that you are not guilty of any sin bad enough to send you to hell. What you need to understand is the fact that, the severity of the sins you are guilty of is irrelevant. Sin is disobeying God's laws and everyone is guilty of that. This makes sins without degree because they are all equal in the fact that we have all disobeyed God at one time or another. Because of this, there is no one innocent; we are all guilty before God. The Bible teaches that man's righteousness is as filthy rags in the sight of God. (Is 64:6) Allow me to illustrate; how many lies does a person have to tell before they are guilty of being a liar? How many sins must a person commit before they are guilty of being a sinner? I think we all know the answer. So how many sins (God's laws) must a person break before they are guilty be of breaking His laws? We need to realize that we were already guilty. Jesus did not come to make us guilty of sin; He came to save us from our sins. (Jn 3:17)

There are those who believe that you can earn your way to heaven by doing good works, or in other words, by keeping God's laws. If that were possible, then it would be true that you could be saved that way, but it isn't possible. The problem is that humans are not capable of keeping God's laws and that is why God gave us the law so we would be able to see our guilt. If we could keep all of the laws we wouldn't need a savior. This would be salvation by good works. The Bible tells us this is not possible.

> *"For by grace are ye saved through faith; and that not of yourselves: it is the gift of God: Not of works, lest any man should boast." (Eph 2:8-9)*

The Bible also teaches us that the wages (payment that we deserve) for being sinners is death.

> "For the wages of sin is death; but the gift of God is eternal life through Jesus Christ our Lord" (Rom 6:23)

What is Spiritual Death?

The word death here means to separate or to take away. When a person dies their spirit separates from their body leaving the body lifeless. When a person dies a spiritual death, then their spirit is separated from the Spirit of God for all eternity. Thus, spiritual life is a description of the joining of God's Spirit with your spirit for eternity. Unfortunately, this means that since the fall of mankind all people are born separated from God and therefore they are born spiritually dead. I will show you that later in the Greek dictionary. In this case it is referring to the separation of your spirit from the presence of God for all of eternity. The laws of God were given to man in order to make us realize that we needed to be saved from ourselves because of what we have done. In this same verse however, it also declares that there still remains a glimmer of hope for man-kind. That is because God is willing to give us a free gift. This free gift that He is offering is eternal life through His Son Jesus Christ. Man-kind does not have the ability to save them-selves, but God has a plan for our salvation. This salvation is a free gift from God and cannot be earned by any man, or woman. Don't try to blame God for the human condition. He has done everything possible to save us.

"For God sent not his Son into the world to condemn the world; but that the world through him might be saved." (Jn 3:17)

"He that believeth on him is not condemned: but he that believeth not is condemned already, because he hath not believed in the name of the only begotten Son of God." (Jn 3:18)

What Does Repentance Mean?

After you realize that you are a sinner and that you stand guilty before God you must feel remorseful for your sins, or sorry that you were unable to remain sinless. This is repentance, it simply means to turn from your sin, without repentance there is no remission of sins, (without repentance sins cannot be forgiven).

"For godly sorrow worketh repentance to salvation not to be repented of: but the sorrow of the world worketh death." (2Cor 7:10)

"The Lord is not slack concerning his promise, as some men count slackness; but is longsuffering to us—ward, not willing that any should perish, but that all should come to repentance." (2Pet 3:9)

"Repent ye therefore, and be converted, that your sins may be blotted out, when

> *the times of refreshing shall come from the presence of the Lord." (Acts 3:19)*

Receive the Free Gift of Eternal Life

After you have repented, now you are prepared to receive the free gift of eternal life. This is accomplished by believing that Jesus is the Son of God and that He came here to earth from heaven to die on the cross in order to pay the price for your sins. This is obviously not the same as just believing that there is a God. It is the act of believing that Jesus Christ is God and that He came here to save you. The devil believes in God and trembles with fear in God's presence.

> *"Thou believest that there is one God; thou doest well: the devils also believe, and tremble." (James 2:19)*

Believing is faith, in other words, believing that Jesus is who He claims to be and that He can do what He says He can do for you. When you repent of your sins and believe in Christ, then all that remains is for you to ask God to save you.

> *"That if thou shalt confess with thy mouth the Lord Jesus, and shalt believe in thine heart that God hath raised him from the dead, thou shalt be saved. For with the heart man believeth unto righteousness; and with the mouth confession is made unto salvation. For the scripture saith, Whosoever believeth on him shall not be*

ashamed. For there is no difference between the Jew and the Greek: for the same Lord over all is rich unto all that call upon him. For whosoever shall call upon the name of the Lord shall be saved." (Rom 10:9-13)

Saving Faith

Faith must be exercised in order to mean anything. If I say that I believe that the old broken down fold up lawn chair out in the back yard will hold me up if I sit on it, well some may believe me and some may not. I may not even believe it can hold me up myself, faith without action is empty. (Jms 2:17) However, if I go and sit on that chair, then I have proven that I have enough faith that I'm willing to trust it, and then the faith means something. If you call on Jesus to save you, then you must exercise your faith and believe in your heart that He did what you asked him to do. When you put your faith in Christ there is no more condemnation, (You are no longer guilty of being a sinner).

> *"But God commendeth his love toward us, in that, while we were yet sinners, Christ died for us." (Rom 5:8)*

After you become a child of God through our Lord Jesus Christ there is no power in heaven, in hell, or on earth that can change that.

> *"For I am persuaded, that neither death, nor life, nor angels, nor principalities, nor powers, nor things present, nor things to come, Nor height, nor depth, nor any other creature, shall be able to separate us from the love of God, which is in Christ Jesus our Lord." (Rom 8:38-39)*

Salvation Cannot Be Lost

Unfortunately however, there are those who would tell you that you can lose your salvation by not following or keeping God's laws. This doesn't even make any sense to me. If there is no good work that I can do that is good enough to save me in the first place, then how are good works going to keep me saved. I personally thank God that my salvation doesn't depend on my ability to keep God's laws. I think I would lose my salvation in the first ten minutes of every day. Good works can't save you, and they can't keep you saved. As long as you have doubts about whether Jesus actually saved you like He said He would, or that you may not be able to stay saved, it limits Gods ability to use you to do His work while you are here on earth. It is God's will for every Christian to become mature in their spiritual life and to serve God in some capacity. In the following chapters of this book the Holy Spirit has inspired me to show you why your salvation is secured in Christ Jesus and if you have accepted Him as your savior, then why you will never be lost again. In the mean time, I would like to encourage anyone who has read this plan of salvation and has not already secured their place in heaven to do so right now. Even if you think you may have gone through all the motions, or said all the words, but you didn't really understand what you were doing at the time, then you should do it again. I don't believe you can get saved unless you understand what you are doing when you do it; I say it is better to know for sure. If you were saved the first time you called on Jesus to save you, then you are just reaffirming your position with God and if you're not sure, then this will give you the assurance that you need to move forward in your Christian life. Just say this simple prayer below. If you say this prayer and you believe that God has saved you like he promised, then you should record this occasion in your Bible. It may be helpful to you in the future when the devil will try to give you doubts.

The Sinners Prayer for Salvation

Heavenly Father, I know that I am a sinner and I cannot go to heaven with my sin. I am sorry for being a sinner and I come to you asking for forgiveness for being a sinner. I believe that Jesus Christ is your Son and that He is God and that you have the authority to forgive me. Lord, please forgive me of my sins and make me a born again child of God. Lord I do believe that you have done what I have asked you to do and from this day forward I want to live a life that is pleasing to you. In Jesus name I pray. AMEN!

Chapter Three

Everlasting Life

Without End or Interruption

I am certain that I am saved and I can never lose my salvation because of the words "everlasting life". In the Greek language the word everlasting is "Aionios", (Ahee-o'-nee-os). This word means perpetual, it is used to represent past, present and future tenses, eternal, forever, perpetuity meaning without end and without interruption. So let me show you how this word is used in relation to salvation in God's Word:

> *"And every one that hath forsaken houses, or brethren, or sisters, or father, or mother, or wife, or children, or lands, for my name's sake, shall receive an hundredfold, and shall inherit everlasting life." (Mtt 19:29)*

"He that believeth on the Son hath everlasting life: and he that believeth not the Son shall not see life; but the wrath of God abideth on him." (Jn 3:36"

"But now being made free from sin, and become servants to God, ye have your fruit unto holiness, and the end everlasting life." (Rom 6:22)

Additional references: Jn 3:16, Lk 18:30, Jn 4:14, Jn 5:24, Jn 6:27, Gal 6:8, I Tim 1:16

Life without End

If it were possible to lose your salvation, then we could not have life without end and if we could get it back again, it would not be life without interruption. Eternal life is therefore, by definition, not possible to lose, and it would also not be possible to re-obtain it, if you could lose it. The best way to clarify what is life according to God, is to explain what is death. The word "death" comes from the Greek word "Apogo" (Ap-ag'-0) which means to depart, separate or take away as I mentioned earlier. When you die your spirit is separated from your body. Since the Bible teaches that life begins at the time of conception, then it is believed that this is when God provides the spirit of life. When you die that spirit of life that God provided at your conception departs the body. The flesh is no longer supported and withers away, the spirit however, lives on for eternity. When our body and spirit are born in the flesh this is the first birth. It is referred to as a water birth. When we are born again is when we receive a second Spirit. This is the Spirit of God that joins with our spirit at the time of our salvation. These spirits are joined like a man and wife, they become one and are inseparable. This is called the second birth, or the spiritual birth. This explains why the Bible teaches that after we are born again we are in God and God is in us, because the Spirit of God that joins with our spirit is God. (1 Jn 4:13-16) We will discuss this more in another chapter.

> *"Jesus answered and said unto him, Verily, verily, I say unto thee, Except a man be born again, he cannot see the kingdom of God. Nicodemus saith unto him, How can a man be born when he is old? can he enter the second time into his mother's womb, and be born? Jesus answered, Verily, verily, I say unto thee, Except a man be born of water and of the Spirit, he cannot enter into the kingdom of God. That which is born of the flesh is flesh; and that which is born of the Spirit is spirit. Marvel not that I said unto thee, Ye must be born again. The wind bloweth where it listeth, and thou hearest the sound thereof, but canst not tell whence it cometh, and whither it goeth: so is every one that is born of the Spirit." (Jn 3:3-8)*

> *"Being born again, not of corruptible seed, but of incorruptible, by the word of*

> *God, which liveth and abideth for ever."*
> *1Pet 1:23)*
>
> *Additional references: Jn 1:13, I Jn 3:9, Gal 4:23 & 4:29, I Jn 2:29, I Jn 4:7, I JN 5:1, 5:4 & 5:8*

It is the joining of our spirit with God's Spirit that make us the children of God. When we die the first death is when our spirits separate from our bodies. For those who never get saved the second death will be when their spirits are separated from God for all eternity, this is called the second death.

When an unsaved person dies their soul goes to a place called hell, a place which was created to hold the devil and his demons. At the great white throne judgment where every soul that ever lived, other than those who have been saved, will be judged, the souls in hell will come before the throne and be judged as well. After this judgment, then the souls that were in hell will be cast into the Lake of Fire for eternity. This is called the second death because this is the eternal separation of the person's spirit from God's presence.

> *"And I saw the dead, small and great, stand before God; and the books were opened: and another book was opened, which is the book of life: and the dead were judged out of those things which were written in the books, according to their works. And the sea gave up the dead which were in it; and death and hell delivered up the dead which*

> *were in them: and they were judged every man according to their works. And death and hell were cast into the lake of fire. This is the second death. And whosoever was not found written in the book of life was cast into the lake of fire." (Rev 20:12-15)*

So you see, he who is born only once must die twice, but he who is born twice must only die once. If you are not born again when you die your spirit will separate from your body when you die and your spirit will be separated from God for eternity when it is cast into the lake of fire. If you are born of the flesh and born again of the spirit then your spirit will separate from your body when you die, but since your spirit is now one with God's Spirit, you will never be separated from God. To sum it all up, If you are born again your salvation is secured for all eternity.

Salvation comes with a Security Deposit

Because of the fact that the Spirit of God is one with your spirit when you are born again this is another reason why your salvation is secured for eternity. Because of the fact the Holy Spirit is given to Christians as a guarantee to you of your eternal inheritance. The gift of the Holy Spirit is referred to as the earnest of our salvation. The Greek word is Arrhabon (Ar-hrab-ohn'). This word means a pledge, a security deposit or a promise that the rest of what you have been guaranteed will come. We will talk about this in detail when we get to the chapter on the Holy Spirit.

> *"Who hath also sealed us, and given the earnest of the Spirit in our hearts. (2Cor 1:22)*
>
> *"Now he that hath wrought us for the selfsame thing is God, who also hath given unto us the earnest of the Spirit." (2Cor 5:5)*
>
> *"In whom ye also trusted, after that ye heard the word of truth, the gospel of your salvation: in whom also after that ye believed, ye were sealed with that holy Spirit of promise, Which is the earnest of our inheritance until the redemption of the purchased possession, unto the praise of his glory." (Eph 1:13-14)*

Essentially the Holy Spirit is God's promise to each born again Christian that they have (not will have), but have inherited eternal life. God cannot lie.

> *"In hope of eternal life, which God, that cannot lie, promised before the world began;" (Tit 1:2)*
>
> *"That by two immutable things, in which it was impossible for God to lie, we might have a strong consolation, who have fled for refuge to lay hold upon the hope set before us:" (Heb 6:18)*

Whenever someone makes a major purchase and they are not going to pay for the whole thing up front, they are generally required to make a security deposit or a down payment. That deposit is a promise that the total price will be paid in full in the future guaranteed. When Jesus died on the cross He paid the full purchase price for our salvation by the shedding of His blood. When we get saved God gives us the Holy Spirit as a down payment promising that we will receive everything that Jesus has paid for.

Chapter Four

The Unpardonable Sin

Only Sin Not Forgivable

There is only one sin that cannot be forgiven. This sin is sometimes referred to as the unpardonable sin, or the blaspheming of the Holy Ghost. This unpardonable sin can only be committed prior to salvation. After you have accepted Christ it would be impossible to deny the Holy Ghost access since He is already inside you.

> *"But he that shall blaspheme against the Holy Ghost hath never forgiveness, but is in danger of eternal damnation." (Mk 3:29)*

The rejection of Christ as your savior is the only sin that cannot be forgiven because it is the only means to salvation. If you reject the gospel (The opportunity to accept Christ as your savior), then you are rejecting or blaspheming the power of the Holy Spirit to indwell you, which is what provides your spirit with eternal life.

> *"He that believeth and is baptized shall be saved; but he that believeth not shall be damned." (Mk 16:16)*

> *"For God sent not his Son into the world to condemn the world; but that the world through him might be saved. He that believeth on him is not condemned: but he that believeth not is condemned already, because he hath not believed in the name of the only begotten Son of God." (Jn 3:17-18)*

The Indwelling of the Spirit

When the Apostles were with Jesus here on the earth, the Holy Spirit did not dwell within them because Jesus had not yet ascended. The ascension of Jesus is referring to the fact that He ascended into heaven forty days after His resurrection. (Acts 1:1-3) After His ascension, He sent the Holy Spirit down from heaven to the Apostles. Since then the Holy Spirit indwells those who believe in Christ and accept Him as their savior. We shall discuss this further in another chapter.

We were all born sinners and are already destined for eternal separation from God as soon as we are born. Only those who have not reached the age of reason, or the age of accountability (The age that one is when they are old enough to comprehend the gospel of salvation and make a decision on whether to believe or not believe) are protected from eternal separation from God for His name sake. "I write unto you, little children, because your sins are forgiven you for his name's sake." (I Jn 2:12)

> *"Wherefore, as by one man sin entered into the world, and death by sin; and so death passed upon all men, for that all have sinned: (For until the law sin was in the world: but sin is not imputed when there is no law. Nevertheless death reigned from Adam to Moses, even over them that had not sinned after the similitude of Adam's transgression, who is the figure of him that was to come. But not as the offence, so also is the free gift. For if through the offence of one many be dead, much more the grace of God, and the gift by grace, which is by one man, Jesus Christ, hath abounded unto many. And not as it was by one that sinned, so is the gift: for the judgment was by one to condemnation, but the free gift is of many offences unto justification. (For if by one man's offence death reigned by one; much more they which receive abundance of grace and of the gift of righteousness shall reign in life by one, Jesus Christ.) Therefore as by the offence of one judgment came upon all men to condemnation; even so by the righteousness of one the free gift came upon all men unto justification of life. For as by one man's disobedience many were made*

> *sinners, so by the obedience of one shall many be made righteous." (Rom 5:12-19)*

Jesus Cannot Deny Himself

One might conclude therefore, that if someone accepts Christ and are born again and yet later they turn back to their old ways, even to the point that they would deny Christ, that they would no longer be saved. This conclusion is inaccurate because once a person has received Christ they become one with Christ and Jesus cannot deny Himself.

> *"It is a faithful saying: For if we be dead with him, we shall also live with him: If we suffer, we shall also reign with him: if we deny him, he also will deny us: If we believe not, yet he abideth faithful: he cannot deny himself." (2Tim 2:11-13)*

In some religions the Apostle Peter is considered to be the foundation of the church. Others believe that Peter's profession of faith, that Jesus is the Son of God, is the foundation that the church was built on.

> *"He saith unto them, But whom say ye that I am? And Simon Peter answered and said, Thou art the Christ, the Son of the living God. And Jesus answered and said unto him, Blessed art thou, Simon Barjona: for flesh and blood hath not revealed it unto thee, but my Father which is in heaven. And I say also unto thee, That thou art Peter, and*

> *upon this rock I will build my church; and the gates of hell shall not prevail against it. And I will give unto thee the keys of the kingdom of heaven: and whatsoever thou shalt bind on earth shall be bound in heaven: and whatsoever thou shalt loose on earth shall be loosed in heaven." (Matt 16:15-19)*

Even Peter the Apostle Denied Christ at one Time

Regardless of what you think these verses mean concerning Peter's part in the establishing of the church, he was chosen by God to be one of the original twelve Apostles and played an important role in starting Jesus' church. He was and still is held in high esteem when it comes to exemplary Christian leaders and he was the one who introduced salvation to the gentiles. God sent Peter a vision that resulted in God telling him that what God has cleansed the Jewish people should not call unclean. God was telling Peter that salvation was for the Jews and the gentiles. In this case a gentile is anyone who was not a Jew. The Jews were God's chosen people and they felt that God's blessings were only for them prior to this time. We will talk more about all of this as well. You can read about this in Acts 10:1-47.

I said all of that to say this: Even though Peter played a fundamental role in establishing the church, he denied Christ three times before his ministry even began, just as Jesus told him he would.

> *"Peter answered and said unto him, Though all men shall be offended because of thee, yet will I never be offended. Jesus said unto him, Verily I say unto thee, That this night, before the cock crow, thou shalt deny me thrice. Peter said unto him, Though I should die with thee, yet will I not deny thee. Likewise also said all the disciples." (Matt 26:33-35)*

> *"Then began he to curse and to swear, saying, I know not the man. And immediately the cock crew. And Peter remembered the word of Jesus, which said unto him, Before the cock crow, thou shalt deny me thrice. And he went out, and wept bitterly." (Matt 26:74-75)*

Additional References: LK 22:34, 61

We know that Peter was a gigantic figure in the beginning of the church and yet he denied knowing Christ three times that we know of and this was even before his ministry began. He obviously did not lose his salvation over this denial. When you are introduced to Christ through the gospel (the plan of salvation), provided you are of sound mind, you can either accept or reject Christ as you savior. If you accept Him, you are saved from then on, even if you deny Christ at a later date. If you deny Him, at the time of the introduction, then you will remain in your current lost (spiritually dead) condition. You may or may not get another opportunity to be saved after that. We are told that every person will eventually have the opportunity to be saved, there is no promise that they will get that chance more than one time. (Matt 24:14)

Chapter Five

Salvation is a Free Gift from God

We Are Not Saved by Our Own Work

Our salvation is secured for eternity because it is a free gift from God to us, we cannot do anything to earn it. If we had to do something to earn it, then it would be reasonable to assume that we would have to keep doing something to keep it.

> *"Whom God hath set forth to be a propitiation through faith in his blood, to declare his righteousness for the remission of sins that are past, through the forbearance of God; To declare, I say, at this time his righteousness: that he might be just, and the justifier of him which believeth in Jesus. Where is boasting then? It is excluded. By what law? of works? Nay: but by the law of*

faith. Therefore we conclude that a man is justified by faith without the deeds of the law. Is he the God of the Jews only? is he not also of the Gentiles? Yes, of the Gentiles also: "Seeing it is one God, which shall justify the circumcision by faith, and uncircumcision through faith." (Rom 3:25-30)

"For if Abraham were justified by works, he hath whereof to glory; but not before God. For what saith the scripture? Abraham believed God, and it was counted unto him for righteousness. Now to him that worketh is the reward not reckoned of grace, but of debt. But to him that worketh not, but believeth on him that justifieth the ungodly, his faith is counted for righteousness. Even as David also describeth the blessedness of the man, unto whom God imputeth righteousness without works," (Rom 4:2-6)

"For by grace are ye saved through faith; and that not of yourselves: it is the gift of God: Not of works, lest any man should boast." (Eph 2:8-9)

If we could earn our salvation by doing good works, or keeping God's laws, then we would not need Jesus to be saved. The Bible makes it clear that no-one is saved by keeping God's laws. There are over 600 laws in the Old Testament and it is not possible for even the most dedicated servant of God to keep them all. The law was given to man in order to point out the fact that we are all sinners and in need of a savior.

> *"Therefore by the deeds of the law there shall no flesh be justified in his sight: for by the law is the knowledge of sin. But now the righteousness of God without the law is manifested, being witnessed by the law and the prophets; Even the righteousness of God which is by faith of Jesus Christ unto all and upon all them that believe: for there is no difference: For all have sinned, and come short of the glory of God; Being justified freely by his grace through the redemption that is in Christ Jesus:" (Rom 3:20-24}*

What Can You Do So Bad that you Lose What You Never Deserved

So let me ask you this; If God gave us something (eternal life) that we never could earn by keeping the law, then how could we lose something (eternal life) we never deserved, by breaking the law that we were never able to keep? The law was not written for the saved (righteous).

> *"For Christ is the end of the law for righteousness to every one that believeth." (Rom 10:4)*

> *"Knowing that a man is not justified by the works of the law, but by the faith of Jesus Christ, even we have believed in Jesus Christ, that we might be justified by the faith of Christ, and not by the works of the law: for by the works of the law shall no flesh be justified." (Gal 2:16)*

> *"But the scripture hath concluded all under sin, that the promise by faith of Jesus Christ might be given to them that believe. But before faith came, we were kept under the law, shut up unto the faith which should afterwards be revealed. Wherefore the law was our schoolmaster to bring us unto Christ, that we might be justified by faith. But after that faith is come, we are no longer under a schoolmaster. For ye are all the children of God by faith in Christ Jesus." (Gal 3:22-26)*

> *"But we know that the law is good, if a man use it lawfully; Knowing this, that the law is not made for a righteous man, but for the lawless and disobedient, for the ungodly and for sinners, for unholy and profane, for murderers of fathers and murderers of mothers, for manslayers, For whoremongers, for them that defile themselves with mankind, for menstealers, for liars, for perjured persons, and if there be any other thing that is contrary to sound doctrine;" (1Tim 1:8-10)*

The law is fulfilled by love. The love that comes from the Spirit of God that resides within you. For love worketh no ill toward its neighbor.

> *"Master, which is the great commandment in the law? Jesus said unto him, Thou shalt love the Lord thy God with all thy heart, and with all thy soul, and with all thy mind. This is the first and great commandment.*

And the second is like unto it, Thou shalt love thy neighbour as thyself. On these two commandments hang all the law and the prophets." (Matt 22:36-40)

We Keep the Laws Because We are Saved

Christians do not keep the laws, or try to do good works in order to be saved, but rather because they are saved. They try to live righteously because they want to live a life that is pleasing to God. If you love God and you love your neighbors, then you will not do anything that would cause them suffering, be it mental or physical. Look at these verses that describe the relationship between love and keeping the law or commandments.

"If ye love me, keep my commandments." (Jn 14:15)

"If ye keep my commandments, ye shall abide in my love; even as I have kept my Father's commandments, and abide in his love." (Jn 15:10)

"But as it is written, Eye hath not seen, nor ear heard, neither have entered into the heart of man, the things which God hath prepared for them that love him." (1Cor 2:9)

"If any man love not the Lord Jesus Christ, let him be Anathema Maranatha." (1Cor 16:22)

"Be ye therefore followers of God, as dear children; And walk in love, as Christ also hath loved us, and hath given himself for us an offering and a sacrifice to God for a sweetsmelling savour. But fornication, and all uncleanness, or covetousness, let it not be once named among you, as becometh saints; Neither filthiness, nor foolish talking, nor jesting, which are not convenient: but rather giving of thanks. For this ye know, that no whoremonger, nor unclean person, nor covetous man, who is an idolater, hath any inheritance in the kingdom of Christ and of God. Let no man deceive you with vain words: for because of these things cometh the wrath of God upon the children of disobedience. Be not ye therefore partakers with them. For ye were sometimes darkness, but the Lord: walk as children of light: (For the fruit of the Spirit is in all goodness and righteousness and truth;) Proving what is acceptable unto the Lord. And have no fellowship with the unfruitful works of darkness, but rather reprove them. For it is a shame even to speak of those things which are done of them in secret." (Eph 5:1-12)

Who is my Neighbor?

Just for clarification, I said that love will cause no harm to his neighbor, therefore it is necessary to understand who is your neighbor. I think this is best illustrated by what Jesus said to His Apostles.

> *"But he, willing to justify himself, said unto Jesus, And who is my neighbour? And Jesus answering said, A certain man went down from Jerusalem to Jericho, and fell among thieves, which stripped him of his raiment, and wounded him, and departed, leaving him half dead. And by chance there came down a certain priest that way: and when he saw him, he passed by on the other side. And likewise a Levite, when he was at the place, came and looked on him, and passed by on the other side. But a certain Samaritan, as he journeyed, came where he was: and when he saw him, he had compassion on him, And went to him, and bound up his wounds, pouring in oil and wine, and set him on his own beast, and brought him to an inn, and took care of him. And on the morrow when he departed, he took out two pence, and gave them to the host, and said unto him, Take care of him; and whatsoever thou spendest more, when I come again, I will repay thee. Which now of these three, thinkest thou, was neighbour unto him that fell among the thieves? And he said, He that shewed mercy on him. Then said Jesus unto him, Go, and do thou likewise." (Luke 10:29-37)*

In this parable it should be pointed out that the two men that past by and did nothing to help were men of status. A priest and a Levite, these were men who were religious leaders; God's chosen people, men with wealth. On the other hand, the man who went above and beyond to help the stranger was a Samaritan. Samaritans were considered to be the low life's of the time. Here is the point; your neighbor is anyone that you see in need regardless of who they are racially, or financially, or religiously. If you have the means to help someone, then you should do it. I'm not just talking about people you are friends with, or fellow Christians, or people that you know. If you see anyone in need, even a perfect stranger and you have the means to help them, then you should do it. This is what God expects His children to do.

To summarize, we cannot lose our salvation by failing to keep God's commandments, or in other words, by doing good works. God's children do good works because they are saved not because they are trying to earn their way to heaven.

Chapter Six

Saved Sinners

Forgiven for Being Sinners

Our salvation is secured for eternity because we were forgiven for being sinners. As I have mentioned previously there are two types of sinners, saved sinners and lost sinners. Christians are saved sinners because they have accepted Jesus Christ as their personal savior. Consider the following verses:

> *"And he spake this parable unto certain which trusted in themselves that they were righteous, and despised others: Two men went up into the temple to pray; the one a Pharisee, and the other a publican. The Pharisee stood and prayed thus with himself, God, I thank thee, that I am not as other men are, extortioners, unjust, adulterers, or even as this publican. I fast twice in the week, I give tithes of all that I*

> *possess. And the publican, standing afar off, would not lift up so much as his eyes unto heaven, but smote upon his breast, saying, God be merciful to me a sinner. I tell you, this man went down to his house justified rather than the other: for every one that exalteth himself shall be abased; and he that humbleth himself shall be exalted." (Luke 18:9-14)*

Forgiven for all of Your Sins

Mercy is God with-holding the punishment that we deserve for being sinners and grace is God giving us the gift of eternal life which we do not deserve. When this publican prayed to God for forgiveness he did not name every sin that he had ever committed and ask for forgiveness for each one individually. He simply asked God to forgive him for being a sinner. Why does this distinction matter? When Christians ask God for salvation, which includes the forgiveness of sins, we don't try to recall ever sin we ever committed, we just ask God to forgive us for being sinners. When we are born in the flesh we are born a sinful birth. When we are born of the Holy Spirit we are born a righteous birth. When Jesus died on the cross which part of your sins did He die for? Did He die to pay for your past, present or future sins? The answer is, He died to pay for all of your sins. When Jesus paid for your sins with His blood all of your sins were future sins because you had obviously not even been born yet.

Therefore He died for all the sins that you will ever commit during your entire life time on earth. When you accepted God's forgiveness, He forgave you for all of your past, present and future sins. If this is true, then any sins that you commit in the future, after you have been saved, have no affect on God's forgiveness, or on your eternal destiny. Never-the-less Christians strive to live righteously because they want to please God. When a Christian sins however, it does grieve the Holy Spirit that lives inside them and causes a break in fellowship between them and God. We do still need to ask God for forgiveness when we sin because this will restore that broken fellowship between us and God and between us and our neighbors. Relationships are not contingent upon harmony whereas fellowship indeed is.

> *"And he said unto them, When ye pray, say, Our Father which art in heaven, Hallowed be thy name. Thy kingdom come. Thy will be done, as in heaven, so in earth. Give us day by day our daily bread. And forgive us our sins; for we also forgive every one that is indebted to us. And lead us not into temptation; but deliver us from evil." (Lk 11:2-4)*

> *"For verily I say unto you, That whosoever shall say unto this mountain, Be thou removed, and be thou cast into the sea; and shall not doubt in his heart, but shall believe that those things which he saith shall come*

to pass; he shall have whatsoever he saith. Therefore I say unto you, What things soever ye desire, when ye pray, believe that ye receive them, and ye shall have them. And when ye stand praying, forgive, if ye have ought against any: that your Father also which is in heaven may forgive you your trespasses. But if ye do not forgive, neither will your Father which is in heaven forgive your trespasses." (Mk 11:23-26)

"Put on therefore, as the elect of God, holy and beloved, bowels of mercies, kindness, humbleness of mind, meekness, longsuffering; Forbearing one another, and forgiving one another, if any man have a quarrel against any even as Christ forgave you, so also do ye." (Col 3:12-13)

God Forgives Sinners Not Sins

It makes sense if you consider the fact that God does not forgive sins, He forgives sinners. As far as our salvation is concerned, all of our sins have been forgiven, but we can't expect to have any closeness to God if we break His laws. All of God's laws deal with two types of responsibilities; first our responsibilities concerning our relationship between us and God, as in the first five of the Ten Commandments, and second, our responsibilities concerning our relationship between us and other people, as in the last five of the Ten Commandments. When we break His laws it affects our fellowship with God and with our neighbors so we need to be forgiven for those sins. (1Jn 1:9) That distinction is somewhat confusing because it is still the sinner that is being forgiven for the sins that he has committed not the sin itself being forgiven.

Chapter Seven

Salvation is a Relationship

Related to God

Notice in the previous chapter I said our responsibilities concerning our relationship with God, not our fellowship. The fact that we are related to God once we become children of God is another reason why our salvation is secured for all eternity. We are born into our earthly families at the time of our first, or natural birth, and we are born into God's family at our second birth, or Spiritual birth when we accept Christ as our personal savior. You can believe the fact that Christ was sent to be the savior of the world without accepting Him as your own personal savior.

> *"Whosoever is born of God doth not commit sin; for his seed remaineth in him: and he*

> *cannot sin, because he is born of God." (Jn 3:9)*
>
> *"Beloved, let us love one another: for love is of God; and every one that loveth is born of God, and knoweth God." (Jn 4:7)*

As a child of your worldly parents you are related by blood. No matter what you do in your life you cannot change who you are related to. As long as you live on earth their blood will run through your veins. You can disown them, you can wish that they never existed, you can deny them, you can hate them, you can refuse to have anything to do with them, but you cannot change the fact that you are related to them by blood. You will always be related to them through your blood and through your DNA. We cannot change who our parents are, or the fact that they will always be related to us. That actually puts a smile on my face because it makes me realize that our relationship to God is the same way. We are blood relation to God the Father through the blood of Jesus Christ because we are one with Him. Once we are saved we have no say so about it. We are God's children born through the Spirit of God and there is nothing we can do to change that. In the verses above it says that the children of God cannot commit sins because we are born of God. This is because all of our sins have been covered from God's sight by the blood of Christ. We are one with Christ and Christ cannot commit sins.

> *"But love ye your enemies, and do good, and lend, hoping for nothing again; and your reward shall be great, and ye shall be the children of the Highest: for he is kind unto the unthankful and to the evil. Be ye therefore merciful, as your Father also is merciful." (Lk 6:35-36)*

> *"The Spirit itself beareth witness with our spirit, that we are the children of God:" (Rom 8:16)*

> *"And it shall come to pass, that in the place where it was said unto them, Ye are not my people; there shall they be called the children of the living God." (Rom 9:26)*

Related by Adoption

If that isn't enough to convince you, then maybe you should know that we are also related to God by adoption. This relationship binds us legally to God with a contract that cannot be broken. Adoption is a relationship that is based on the legal system. That means that as far as the law is concerned, this relationship is even more binding than one of blood. What a wonderful and glorious thing it is to realize that we are God's children and are therefore entitled to all the rights of son ship.

> *"But when the fulness of the time was come, God sent forth his Son, made of a woman, made under the law, To redeem them that*

> *were under the law, that we might receive the adoption of sons. And because ye are sons, God hath sent forth the Spirit of his Son into your hearts, crying, Abba, Father. Wherefore thou art no more a servant, but a son; and if a son, then an heir of God through Christ." (Gal 4:4-7)*
>
> *"Having predestinated us unto the adoption of children by Jesus Christ to himself, according to the good pleasure of his will," (Eph 1:5)*

The word adoption here is translated from the Greek word "Huiothesia" (hwee-oth-es-ee'-ah). It means the placing of a son, son ship in respect to God. So therefore we are related to God physically, spiritually and legally. That covers all the bases as there is no other way to be related. As children of God we are heirs to God and all that He possesses. This includes a relationship to the children of Israel (God's chosen people) and all the promises that God made to them as well. God is not a man that He can break His promises. Praise the Lord as children of God we know this is not our final home. God has prepared a place for us in His heavenly domain and we are just passing through this journey of physical life on our way to eternity.

A Child Of Mine

I will lend you, for a little time,
A child of mine, He said.
For you to love the while he lives,
And mourn for when he's dead.
It may be six or seven years,
Or twenty-two or three.
But will you, till I call him back,
Take care of him for Me?
He'll bring his charms to gladden you,
And should his stay be brief.
You'll have his lovely memories,
As solace for your grief.
I cannot promise he will stay,
Since all from earth return.
But there are lessons taught down there,
I want this child to learn.
I've looked the wide world over,
In search for teachers true.
And from the throngs that crowd life's lanes,
I have selected you.
Now will you give him all your love,
Nor think the labour vain.
Nor hate me when I come
To take him home again?
I fancied that I heard them say,
'Dear Lord, Thy will be done!'
For all the joys Thy child shall bring,
The risk of grief we'll run.
We'll shelter him with tenderness,
We'll love him while we may,

And for the happiness we've known,
Forever grateful stay.
But should the angels call for him,
Much sooner than we've planned.
We'll brave the bitter grief that comes,
And try to understand.

Source: By Edgar Allen Guest from familyfriendspoem.com

This not our home, we are only here for a short time compared to eternity. We are God's children and He will bring us home. The security of my salvation is not mine to hold. As a child of God eternal life is part of my inheritance. I am related to God by birth, by blood, by DNA, by marriage and by adoption.

Chapter Eight

God's Omnipotence

God is all Powerful

Our salvation is secured for all eternity because of God's omnipotence. God is all powerful and He is the one that holds on to our salvation. I am saying that God is the one who keeps our salvation secure for us. We cannot keep our salvation any more than we could earn it in the first place. It is given to us by God and kept secure for us by God.

> *"To an inheritance incorruptible, and undefiled, and that fadeth not away, reserved in heaven for you, Who are kept by the power of God through faith unto salvation ready to be revealed in the last time."(1 Pet 1:4-5)*

> *"For whom he did foreknow, he also did predestinate to be conformed to the image*

of his Son, that he might be the firstborn among many brethren. Moreover whom he did predestinate, them he also called: and whom he called, them he also justified: and whom he justified, them he also glorified. What shall we then say to these things? If God be for us, who can be against us? He that spared not his own Son, but delivered him up for us all, how shall he not with him also freely give us all things? Who shall lay any thing to the charge of God's elect? It is God that justifieth. Who is he that condemneth? It is Christ that died, yea rather, that is risen again, who is even at the right hand of God, who also maketh intercession for us. Who shall separate us from the love of Christ? shall tribulation, or distress, or persecution, or famine, or nakedness, or peril, or sword? As it is written, For thy sake we are killed all the day long; we are accounted as sheep for the slaughter. Nay, in all these things we are more than conquerors through him that loved us. For I am persuaded, that neither death, nor life, nor angels, nor principalities, nor powers, nor things present, nor things to come, Nor height, nor depth, nor any other creature, shall be able to separate us from the love of God, which is in Christ Jesus our Lord." (Rom 8:29-39)

"And Jesus said unto them, I am the bread of life: he that cometh to me shall never hunger; and he that believeth on me shall never thirst. But I said unto you, That ye also have seen me, and believe not. All that

the Father giveth me shall come to me; and him that cometh to me I will in no wise cast out. For I came down from heaven, not to do mine own will, but the will of him that sent me. And this is the Father's will which hath sent me, that of all which he hath given me I should lose nothing, but should raise it up again at the last day. And this is the will of him that sent me, that every one which seeth the Son, and believeth on him, may have everlasting life: and I will raise him up at the last day." (Jn 6:35-40)

No More Sacrifice Required

When you accepted Christ as your savior, from that moment on you have belonged to Jesus. In these verses Jesus says that Christians were given to Him by His Father, God the Father. No-one can ever take you away from God the Father because He is all-powerful (Omnipotent). No-one will take you away from Jesus because He promises that whoever is given to Him by His Father He will not lose a single one. He also says He will not cast them out. To me these verses should not even require an explanation. Not only is it not possible for God to lose any of His children, it is not possible for Him to throw any of them back. This certainly sounds like my salvation is secure to me. The main reason that this is necessary is also another reason why we can't lose our salvation and that is because Jesus was the final sacrifice for all sins. Jesus, became the perfect righteous sacrifice to the Father to pay for the sins of mankind with a sufficient sacrifice acceptable to the Father. The Bible says Jesus is the propitiation for our sins. Propitiation means it was a satisfying sacrifice to the Father for the price that had to be paid for the redemption of mankind. (1 Jn 2:2) Jesus is our high priest that intercedes between us and the Father for the forgiveness of our sins on a continual basis and therefore no more sacrifice is needed. There is no more sacrifice required for sins because Jesus satisfied God the Father's requirement needed for the reconciliation of man to God for our atonement. When the Bible states that Jesus is the propitiation for our sins it means that He was the sacrifice that God the Father deemed to be an acceptable sacrifice to satisfy the requirements to pay the debt that was owed.

> *"Whereupon neither the first testament was dedicated without blood. For when Moses had spoken every precept to all the people according to the law, he took the blood of calves and of goats, with water, and scarlet wool, and hyssop, and sprinkled both the book, and all the people, Saying, This is the blood of the testament which God hath enjoined unto you. Moreover he sprinkled with blood both the tabernacle, and all the vessels of the ministry. And almost all things are by the law purged with blood; and without shedding of blood is no remission. It was therefore necessary that the patterns of things in the heavens should*

be purified with these; but the heavenly things themselves with better sacrifices than these. For Christ is not entered into the holy places made with hands, which are the figures of the true; but into heaven itself, now to appear in the presence of God for us: Nor yet that he should offer himself often, as the high priest entereth into the holy place every year with blood of others; For then must he often have suffered since the foundation of the world: but now once in the end of the world hath he appeared to put away sin by the sacrifice of himself. And as it is appointed unto men once to die, but after this the judgment: So Christ was once offered to bear the sins of many; and unto them that look for him shall he appear the second time without sin unto salvation." (Heb 9:18-28)

Throughout the Old Testament sacrifices were made continuously for the remission of the sins of God's chosen people. As you have read without the shedding of blood there is no remission of sins. Jesus was the final sacrifice for the remission of sins for all those who believe in Him and call upon His name for salvation. There are no more sacrifices because Jesus already paid the price for all sins (past, present and future). This sacrifice was made by Christ to make reconciliation of man to God available to the whole world not just the Jewish people.

> *"Even us, whom he hath called, not of the Jews only, but also of the Gentiles? As he saith also in Osee, I will call them my people, which were not my people; and her beloved, which was not beloved. And it shall come to pass, that in the place where it was said unto them, Ye are not my people; there shall they be called the children of the living God."*
> *(Rom 9:24-26)*

Heaven and the Lake of Fire are Both Eternal Destinations

When God the Father looks down on mankind He sees the sins of man, but for Christians He only sees the blood of His Son whose blood was spilt in order to cover the sins of the world to anyone who believes. There remains no other way to have your sins forgiven, or covered, other than by the blood of the lamb. Either you are forgiven through the blood of Christ or you remain destined for eternal damnation for rejecting the sacrifice that God made for you. This last sacrifice illustrates the finality of eternal life or eternal separation from God. You really have no say so about your final destiny once you choose to accept or deny this sacrificial offering as the atonement for your sins. Either you believe and accept and spend eternity with God, or you refuse to believe, and reject it, and spend eternity in hell and the lake of fire. Hell was created for the devil and his angels not for man, never-the-less those who reject God's offer of salvation through the blood of Jesus Christ His Son will spend eternity there. Hell is where those spirits that have left their bodies, which is the first death, will go until the final judgment at the Great White Throne, at which time they will then be cast into the Lake of Fire, which is the second death. The following verses are some of the Bible passages that describe hell and the lake of fire.

> *"And it came to pass, that the beggar died, and was carried by the angels into Abraham's bosom: the rich man also died, and was buried, And in hell he lift up his eyes, being in torments, and seeth Abraham afar off, and Lazarus in his bosom. And he cried and said, Father Abraham, have mercy on me, and send Lazarus, that he may dip the tip of his finger in water, and cool my tongue; for I am tormented in this flame. But Abraham said, Son, remember that thou in thy lifetime receivedst thy good things, and likewise Lazarus evil things: but now he is comforted, and thou art tormented. And beside all this, between us and you there is a great gulf fixed: so that they which would pass from hence to you cannot; neither can they pass to us, that would come from thence. Then he said, I pray thee therefore, father, that thou wouldest send him to my father's house: For I have five brethren; that he may testify unto them, lest they also come into this place of torment." (Lk 16:22-28)*

In the above verses we learn that Abraham's bosom (otherwise known as paradise Lk 23:43) was located in the lower parts of the earth according to Eph 4:9-10 prior to Jesus' ascension into heaven. That is when He made the way to heaven possible. The Old Testament saints were held there in Abraham's bosom until Jesus took them to heaven. There was a great gulf fix that separated hell from paradise. Hell was the holding place for the condemned souls and was also located in the lower parts of the earth. Since the resurrection and ascension of Christ had no affect on the lost souls we would have to assume that these souls are still being held in this temporary place of torment. These verses also tell us that not only is it a place of torment, but there is extreme thirst and heat and flames. It further explains that it is not possible for anyone who has been condemned to ever have a chance to be saved after they have died. It is also not possible for anyone who has been saved to ever be lost again.

> *"And if thy hand offend thee, cut it off: it is better for thee to enter into life maimed, than having two hands to go into hell, into the fire that never shall be quenched: Where their worm dieth not, and the fire is not quenched. And if thy foot offend thee, cut it off: it is better for thee to enter halt into life, than having two feet to be cast into hell, into the fire that never shall be quenched: Where their worm dieth not, and the fire is not quenched. And if thine eye*

> *offend thee, pluck it out: it is better for thee to enter into the kingdom of God with one eye, than having two eyes to be cast into hell fire: Where their worm dieth not, and the fire is not quenched." (Mk 9:43-48)*

In the verses above, Jesus reveals to us a little more information about this place called hell. He tells us it would be better to lose a hand or a foot or even an eye and go to heaven than to go to hell and suffer with all of your body parts. He tells us that in hell there is a fire that is never quenched (never goes out) indicating that the pain never stops. He also says the worm dieth not meaning that the people there will be in so much agony that they will want to die, but they aren't allowed to.

> *"But the children of the kingdom shall be cast out into outer darkness: there shall be weeping and gnashing of teeth." (Matt 8:12)*
>
> *"And fear not them which kill the body, but are not able to kill the soul: but rather fear him which is able to destroy both soul and body in hell." (Matt 10:28)*

In these verses we are told that we should not fear what man will say or do to us if we choose to serve God instead of conforming to what the world thinks we should do or be. We should be more concerned about pleasing God who is able to not only destroy the body which is just temporary, but also the soul which will live in heaven or in hell for all eternity. In Matthew 8:12 we are told that those who are thrown out of the kingdom of heaven will be cast into a place of outer darkness (the absence of light because God is light emphasizing separation from God) and there will be weeping or crying and gnashing of teeth. Gnashing of teeth means to grind your teeth together in pain, sorrow or anger. I believe in this case it refers to all three. It is really quite simple; Jesus made the ultimate sacrifice for all of your sins already. If you believe this is true and accept Him as your savior, and then you are saved and kept saved by the power of God and not by anything you can do. Hell is the alternative; there is no other way to escape damnation because Jesus is the last sacrifice that God will accept. After seeing the descriptions of hell the choice should be clear. The point is that Jesus was and is man's only hope for an escape from eternal separation from God which begins in hell at the time of physical death and is finalized when death and hell are cast into the lake of fire for eternity. If death or separation from God is eternal and life or living in heaven in the presence of God is eternal then salvation has to be eternal also and therefore it cannot be lost.

CHAPTER NINE

The Bride of Christ

Christians are the Bride of Christ

Our salvation is eternally secure because the church (the body of all born again believers) is the bride of Christ. (Eph 5:22-33) I made sure to clarify that by the church I mean all born again believers. This is referred to as the Universal Church. I'm not talking about being a member of a local church, although I believe that you should be, but belonging to, or attending a local church, doesn't make you a part of the Universal Church. You are only part of the Universal Church if you are a born again Christian. (Jn 3:3-5) The word Christian means to be Christ like or to be a follower of Christ. (Acts 11:26) Jesus said you shall know them by their fruits. That means that if you have been saved and are now a child of God, then people should be able see it in the way you live.

> *"Ye shall know them by their fruits. Do men gather grapes of thorns, or figs of thistles? Even so every good tree bringeth forth good fruit; but a corrupt tree bringeth forth evil fruit. A good tree cannot bring forth evil fruit, neither can a corrupt tree bring forth good fruit. Every tree that bringeth not forth good fruit is hewn down, and cast into the fire. Wherefore by their fruits ye shall know them. Not every one that saith unto me, Lord, Lord, shall enter into the kingdom of heaven; but he that doeth the will of my Father which is in heaven. Many will say to me in that day, Lord, Lord, have we not prophesied in thy name? and in thy name have cast out devils? and in thy name done many wonderful works? And then will I profess unto them, I never knew you: depart from me, ye that work iniquity."*
> *(Matt 7:16-23)*

Being Saved is not the result of Being a Good Person

This is not someone who just attends church services or just believes that there is a god. There are many people who are religious, but still lost. They think going to a church makes them good people. Being a good person in the eyes of man is a good thing, but that doesn't make you a good person in the eyes of God. More often than not, being a good person in the eyes of man means to accept everyone for who they are as they like to say. Accepting everyone as they are is denying that there is right and wrong in the world. If we accept everyone as they are then sin is allowed and should not be recognized as wrong or immoral. If we recognize sin is unrighteousness then we cannot accept everyone as being good. Accepting everyone as they are is humanism and therefore placing the rights of man above the commandments of God. I'm talking about a person who has accepted Christ as their personal savior and lives a righteous lifestyle based on God's Word. You can tell it by the way they live. Those who are called the bride of Christ are also sometimes called the body of Christ.

> *"For the husband is the head of the wife, even as Christ is the head of the church: and he is the saviour of the body. Therefore as the church is subject unto Christ, so let the wives be to their own husbands in every thing. Husbands, love your wives, even as Christ also loved the church, and gave himself for it; That he might sanctify and cleanse it with the washing of water by the word, That he might present it to himself a glorious church, not having spot, or wrinkle, or any such thing; but that it should be holy and without blemish. So ought men to love their wives as their own bodies. He that loveth his wife loveth himself. For no man ever yet hated his own flesh; but nourisheth and cherisheth it, even as the Lord the church: For we are members of his body, of his flesh, and of his bones. For this cause shall a man leave his father*

> *and mother, and shall be joined unto his wife, and they two shall be one flesh. This is a great mystery: but I speak concerning Christ and the church." (Eph 5:23-32)*
>
> *Additional References: Col 1:12-20, Eph 1:19-23*

The Marriage Bond is for Life

It may seem strange to say that the church is the bride of Christ and also the body of Christ, but considering the institution of marriage, this is not strange at all. When two people get married they become one flesh just as when you get saved your spirit and the Spirit of God become one spirit. Through the institution of marriage we have become one with Christ just as He is one with the Father. (Jn 10:30) The scriptures make it clear that the marriage bond is intended to be for life. The man is the head and the wife is the body. What happens when the head is removed from the body? The head (man) cannot be removed from the body (the wife) and the head (Jesus) cannot be removed from the body (the church) therefore salvation cannot be lost.

> *"Wherefore they are no more twain, but one flesh. What therefore God hath joined together, let not man put asunder." (Matt 19:6)*

Moses allowed men to give their wives a bill of divorcement because the unfaithful husbands were causing their wives to be abandoned and were forbidden to re-marry. Leave it to man to find ways around doing what is right. Regardless, marriage is intended to last for the remainder of you fleshly life, just as our marriage to Christ is intended to last for the remainder of our spiritual life, which is for eternity.

> *"Meats for the belly, and the belly for meats: but God shall destroy both it and them. Now the body is not for fornication, but for the Lord; and the Lord for the body. And God hath both raised up the Lord, and will also raise up us by his own power. Know ye not that your bodies are the members of Christ? shall I then take the members of Christ, and make them the members of an harlot? God forbid. What? know ye not that he which is joined to an harlot is one body? for two, saith he, shall be one flesh. But he that is joined unto the Lord is one spirit. Flee fornication. Every sin that a man doeth is without the body; but he that committeth fornication sinneth against his own body. What? know ye not that your body is the temple of the Holy Ghost which is in you, which ye have of God, and ye are not your own? For ye are bought with a price: therefore glorify God in your body, and in your spirit, which are God's." (1Cor 6:13-20)*

In our traditional wedding ceremony the father gives away the bride, so it is that God the Father of all born again believers gives Jesus His bride as well. Just as Paul says the husband should be willing to sacrifice his life for his wife, Jesus gave His life for the church. Since we are one with Christ through marriage, which is why we are called the bride of Christ, and the sons of God. Jesus is the son of God and if we are one with Christ then we are the sons of God. Because Jesus is the Lamb of God that died on the cross for our sins Christians are also called the bride of the Lamb.

> *"And there came unto me one of the seven angels which had the seven vials full of the seven last plagues, and talked with me, saying, Come hither, I will shew thee the bride, the Lamb's wife." (Rev 21:9)*

The Lambs bride, or wife, will dwell in the new Jerusalem with Jesus who is the light thereof. Only the bride (those written in the Lambs book of life) will be allowed to enter. Moses may have allowed a bill of divorcement because of man's corruption, but there will be no corruption in heaven. A marriage vow is a promise and God doesn't break His promises. A few months after my wife and I were first married, she asked me what would happen if after a while I decided that I didn't like her any more. Of course, I said that's not going to happen. She replied yea ok, but what if it does. I have never been that good at words especially when put on the spot. I answered; well, a man has to live with his choices. I still hear about that answer regularly. What I meant to say was that the marriage institution is sacred and no matter what, I will not break my promise to her. Not only that, but this is a promise that I made, not only to her, but a promise I made to God as well. I will not break my promise to my wife or God and God will not break His promise to His wife the church or the individual believer.

Chapter Ten

No Condemnation

God Doesn't Threaten People with the Loss of Salvation

I believe salvation is secured for eternity because God never threatens anyone with the loss of salvation in His Word. There will be a judgment where every person shall give an account for their actions in this life, but for Christians the judgment seat of Christ is only for the purpose of the distribution of rewards. Those who have been redeemed by the blood of the lamb are never threatened with punishment of any kind because they are now innocent in the sight of God. For those who believe there is no more condemnation. (Rom 8:1-3)

> *"For other foundation can no man lay than that is laid, which is Jesus Christ. Now if any man build upon this foundation gold, silver,*

precious stones, wood, hay, stubble; Every man's work shall be made manifest: for the day shall declare it, because it shall be revealed by fire; and the fire shall try every man's work of what sort it is. If any man's work abide which he hath built thereupon, he shall receive a reward. If any man's work shall be burned, he shall suffer loss: but he himself shall be saved; yet so as by fire. Know ye not that ye are the temple of God, and that the Spirit of God dwelleth in you? If any man defile the temple of God, him shall God destroy; for the temple of God is holy, which temple ye are." (1Cor 3:11-17)

Additional References: MT 10:40-42, MK 9:41, LK 6:20-23 & 35,

Your Body is the Temple of God

I should point out here, that verse seventeen declares that if a Christian defiles his temple, then God says He will destroy it. Your body is the temple of God if you are saved because the Holy Spirit lives inside your body. This is because when you were saved (born of the Spirit) the Spirit of God joined with your spirit and so now your spirit is one with God's Spirit. We are going to discuss this in more detail later on, but what it is saying is, if you defile your body, then God will destroy your body. This is not the loss of your salvation. God does not threaten to take His Spirit back away from you. You cannot be unborn from your natural birth and you cannot be unborn from your

Spiritual birth either. Notice it clearly states that this person who's body is destroyed, he himself shall be saved in verse thirteen. This is God saying I'm your Father, I brought you in this world and I can take you out. This is the destruction of the body only not the spirit. Following is a list of the five different rewards that are mentioned in the Bible.

> **The crown of righteousness-** *Given to those who love Jesus' appearing. (2Tim 4:8)*
>
> **The imperishable crown-** *Given to those who run a disciplined race. (1Cor 9:24-25)*
>
> **The crown of rejoicing-** *Given to those who rejoice in the Lord's coming. (1Thes 2:19)*
>
> **The crown of life-** *Given to those who are tried by temptation and able to resist it because of their love for Christ. (Jms 1:12)*
>
> **The crown of glory-** *Given to the elders (church leaders) who are faithful to feed the flock (teach the Word to their congregations). (I Pet 5:4)*

There is no explanation as to exactly what these crowns will be like, but the Greek word is "Stephanos" (stef'-an-os) which means; a badge of royalty, a prize or symbol of honor, more elaborate than a simple reward. In any case, the thing that you need to see here is that our salvation is secure because we are the bride of Christ and with God there is no such thing as a divorce.

As previously stated; our salvation is secure because Christians are the temple of God. I briefly mentioned this earlier, but I want to place some more emphasis on this point. In the Old Testament the temple of God (the place where God dwells) was a Holy temple built by the Israelites where only the high priest was allowed to enter. By the way, the word "Holy", simply means set aside for God's purposes. Only the high priest was allowed to enter into the inner most parts of the temple in order to intercede for God's chosen people. It was his job to make the sacrifices brought to him by the people acceptable to God for the forgiveness of their sins. When Jesus died on the cross the veil that separated the outer part of the temple from the altar, where the sacrifices were made, was torn open. This was done to show that there needed to be no more sacrifices for one thing. But also this was done to show that now anyone who would trust in Christ would have direct access to God. This is because the indwelling of the Holy Spirit inside believers makes them the new temple of God. God does not dwell in houses or buildings any longer, He lives inside each Christian and so they have continual access to Him anytime they want.

> *"Jesus, when he had cried again with a loud voice, yielded up the ghost. And, behold, the veil of the temple was rent in twain from the*

top to the bottom; and the earth did quake, and the rocks rent;" (Matt 27:50-51)

"Who found favour before God, and desired to find a tabernacle for the God of Jacob. But Solomon built him an house. Howbeit the most High dwelleth not in temples made with hands; as saith the prophet, Heaven is my throne, and earth is my footstool: what house will ye build me? saith the Lord: or what is the place of my rest? Hath not my hand made all these things?" (Acts 7:46-50)

"Whosoever shall confess that Jesus is the Son of God, God dwelleth in him, and he in God. And we have known and believed the love that God hath to us. God is love; and he that dwelleth in love dwelleth in God, and God in him." (Jn 4:15-15)

Access to God Anytime

I think it is a significant statement to make, the fact that because we are God's temple we have continual access to Him anytime we like. I have been asked numerous times how often do I pray? Do I have certain times set aside for prayer? How important is prayer to me? Let me just say that prayer is very important, but I don't know how to answer these other questions because I learned a long time ago to keep my channel of communication with God open at all times. This allows me to make a quick prayer to God anytime without having to go through a ritual.

That may sound irreverent to some, but it is not intended to be. God is my Father and He wants me to have a close personal relationship with Him. When I talked to my earthly father I was not required to go through a ritual to speak to him and I don't believe God wants us to have to do that either. I like to think of it as personal relationship and not irreverent at all. I talk to God all the time throughout the day. But more importantly, I listen for God's voice all day long every day. When I am about to be tempted to do something questionable I don't have to get on my knees and ask God what He thinks. He tells me before I even give it much thought. If I see someone in need, I don't have to ask God what I should do. He doesn't pull any punches either. His voice, His guidance and His direction are loud and clear to me. There certainly isn't anything wrong with setting aside a dedicated time to talk to God, He might not hear from some of His children at all if they didn't do that, but I think if you realize that you can have continual access to Him anytime you want, then you won't necessarily need to.

Now I'm going to throw in something else here about prayer that is totally free. This may sound strange, but God talks to me in King James English. Jesus told us that the Holy Spirit would bring all things that He had told us to remembrance at the time that we needed it. (Jn 14:26) I have done all of my reading and studying of God's Word in the King James Bible. I'm not going to go into all the reasons why I do that right now. Never-the-less, the thing that I'm trying to explain is when God talks to me it is generally by the method of the Holy Spirit reminding me of something God has already told me before. This is why you need to study, be familiar with, meditate and memorize God's Word, so the Holy Spirit will have plenty of material to work with when God needs to talk to you. I believe the fact that He talks to me in King James makes it easier for me to recognize His words. The Word of God does say pray without ceasing.

> *"Now we exhort you, brethren, warn them that are unruly, comfort the feebleminded, support the weak, be patient toward all men. See that none render evil for evil unto any man; but ever follow that which is good, both among yourselves, and to all men. Rejoice evermore. Pray without ceasing. In every thing give thanks: for this is the will of God in Christ Jesus concerning you." (1Thes 5:14-18)*

Salvation is secure because the Christian's body is God's new home and He has no intentions on giving up His body to live in houses or temples made by men ever again.

Chapter Eleven

A Gift from the Father

A Gift from the Father to the Son

Our salvation is safe forever because we are a gift from God the Father, to God the Son, through the power of God the Holy Spirit. First, I want to make it perfectly clear that there is only one God. (Is 44:6, 1Cor 8:6) God does however exist in three separate parts, the Father, the Son and the Holy Ghost as is made evident when Jesus said you should baptize believers in the names of all three parts. (Matt 28:19) The following verses make it clear that spiritually speaking the children of God have only one Father.

> *"And greetings in the markets, and to be called of men, Rabbi, Rabbi. But be not ye called Rabbi: for one is your Master, even Christ; and all ye are brethren. And call no man your father upon the earth: for one is*

> *your Father, which is in heaven. Neither be ye called masters: for one is your Master, even Christ." (Matt 23:7-10)*

The point I'm trying to make with these verses is that there is only one God, but I would just like to mention that Jesus was pretty specific here when He said call no man Father other than your Father in heaven and yet many religious organizations call their pastors father. Jesus was obviously speaking in religious terms here and saying not to do this when addressing your spiritual leaders. Certainly it is alright to call your earthly father by his proper title because Jesus also said to honor your fathers and mothers. (Eph 6:2-3) I believe Jesus pointed this out because it is important to recognize that there is only one Father spiritually speaking and that is Jehovah. Now look at these verses which support this conclusion.

> *"And Jesus said unto him, Why callest thou me good? there is none good but one, that is, God." (Mk 10:18)*

> *"And Jesus answered him, The first of all the commandments is, Hear, O Israel; The Lord our God is one Lord: And thou shalt love the Lord thy God with all thy heart, and with all thy soul, and with all thy mind, and with all thy strength: this is the first commandment. And the second is like, namely this, Thou shalt love thy neighbour as thyself. There is none other commandment greater than*

> these. And the scribe said unto him, Well, Master, thou hast said the truth: for there is one God; and there is none other but he: And to love him with all the heart, and with all the understanding, and with all the soul, and with all the strength, and to love his neighbour as himself, is more than all whole burnt offerings and sacrifices." (Mk 12:29-33)

One God, Three Parts

Even though there is only one God, He consists of three separate parts. This is called the trinity. He is a triune God. He is also referred to as being a trichotomy which basically means three in one. Man was created in God's image and so we are trichotomies also. Man consist of three parts, the body (flesh and bone), the soul (which is your personality or individuality), and your spirit (breath of life). God is three parts as well, God the Father (the personality), God the Son (the body of God) and God the Holy Spirit (the Spirit of God). Jesus is the body of God. In other words, Jesus is the manifestation of God. That is the part of God that made it possible for man to know God. Manifestation means to make known. (Col 1:15) Jesus is God and was there when the world was created. All things were created by Him and for Him. Jesus is also the word of God. When God spoke the world into existence it was the voice of Jesus. Jesus was the part of God that man was allowed to see on earth. In other words, He was the manifestation of God in the flesh. It is true that the Bible says that God is a Spirit and that no man hath seen Him at any time. (Jn 4:24, Jn 1:18) But that doesn't mean God can't make it possible for us to see the part of Him that He wants us to see. In the Old Testament God revealed His presence in a burning bush and in a cloud of smoke. Jesus is how God chose to reveal Himself to the world in the New Testament. Man also has a part of himself that cannot be seen. My flesh and bone is not what makes me who I am, it is just the vessel that holds my soul. It is my soul that makes me the person that I am. That is why when people look at my body they do not see the part of me that makes me an individual that is different from everyone else. When people see my body they do not see my soul and yet when they see my body they are seeing the part of me that can be seen.

> *"In the beginning was the Word, and the Word was with God, and the Word was God. The same was in the beginning with God. All things were made by him; and without him was not any thing made that as made." (Jn 1:1-3)*

> *"And the Word was made flesh, and dwelt among us, (and we beheld his glory, the glory as of the only begotten of the Father,) full of grace and truth." (Jn 1:14) "Beware lest any man spoil you through philosophy and vain deceit, after the tradition of men, after the rudiments of the world, and not*

after Christ. For in him dwelleth all the fulness of the Godhead bodily."(Col 2:8-9)

I think you can all understand what I am saying by now, but I will give you one more simple illustration. Take an apple for example; it consists of three separate parts, the skin, the meat and the core. Yet with it all together it is still just one apple.

All Three Parts of God Keep Your Salvation Safe

I said all of that to say this; All three parts of God worked together to provide you with eternal life and all three parts of God continue to work together to keep you saved. That is God's job not yours. God the Father sent His Son Jesus, to be a sacrifice for your sins, but God the Father also gave you to His Son in order for you to be saved. For this reason I told you earlier that if you are looking for spiritual answers this is why; God the Father has been trying to lead you to His Son Jesus. If you accept Christ as your savior it is because the Father led you to the Son and gave you to Him as a gift because of the sacrifice that He made to save your soul.

> *"All that the Father giveth me shall come to me; and him that cometh to me I will in no wise cast out. For I came down from heaven, not to do mine own will, but the will of him that sent me. And this is the Father's will which hath sent me, that of*

> *all which he hath given me I should lose nothing, but should raise it up again at the last day. And this is the will of him that sent me, that every one which seeth the Son, and believeth on him, may have everlasting life: and I will raise him up at the last day." (Jn 6:37-40)*

The Holy Spirit is a Gift from God for the purpose of keeping you saved

This offering of your soul to Christ as a gift from God the Father is also revealed in the gift of the Holy Spirit that is given by the Father to those who call upon Him in the name of Jesus for salvation.

> *"Or what man is there of you, whom if his son ask bread, will he give him a stone? Or if he ask a fish, will he give him a serpent? If ye then, being evil, know how to give good gifts unto your children, how much more shall your Father which is in heaven give good things to them that ask him?" (Matt 7:9-11)*

> *"And I say unto you, Ask, and it shall be given you; seek, and ye shall find; knock, and it shall be opened unto you. For every one that asketh receiveth; and he that seeketh findeth; and to him that knocketh it shall be opened. If a son shall ask bread of any of you that is a father, will he give him a stone? or if he ask a fish, will he for a fish give him a serpent? Or if he shall ask an egg, will he offer him a scorpion? If ye then,*

> *being evil, know how to give good gifts unto your children: how much more shall your heavenly Father give the Holy Spirit to them that ask him?" (Lk 11:9-13)*

Even as worldly fathers, we know how to give good gifts to our children. We also know that once you give something to your children it is theirs. You never take back something that you give your child. Actually you should never take back anything that you give to anyone. Now, we may take it away from them for a while for disciplinary reasons, but the child never loses ownership. This is also what happens when we are disobedient to God our Spiritual Father. When we sin we lose that close fellowship with the Father because we are being disciplined, but we do not lose our salvation. Incidentally, it should be noticed that the reason we pray in Jesus' name is because we are one with Jesus and so when we pray to God the Father it is just like Jesus, (God's Son), asking His Father, (God the Father), for whatever it is we are praying for. I have heard some people say that you should never ask God for anything for yourself. That is silly. God is my Father and He expects me to ask Him for things. When I pray I talk to God just like I did when I talked to my earthly father. I say in Jesus' name because it is through Jesus that I have gained access to the Father.

> *"Fear not, little flock; for it is your Father's good pleasure to give you the kingdom." (Lk 12:32)*

"My sheep hear my voice, and I know them, and they follow me: And I give unto them eternal life; and they shall never perish, neither shall any man pluck them out of my hand. My Father, which gave them me, is greater than all; and no man is able to pluck them out of my Father's hand. I and my Father are one." (Jn 10:27-30)

"If ye love me, keep my commandments. And I will pray the Father, and he shall give you another Comforter, that he may abide with you for ever; Even the Spirit of truth; whom the world cannot receive, because it seeth him not, neither knoweth him: but ye know him; for he dwelleth with you, and shall be in you. I will not leave you comfortless: I will come to you. Yet a little while, and the world seeth me no more; but ye see me: because I live, ye shall live also. At that day ye shall know that I am in my Father, and ye in me, and I in you." (Jn 14:15-20)

"These words spake Jesus, and lifted up his eyes to heaven, and said, Father, the hour is come; glorify thy Son, that thy Son also may glorify thee: As thou hast given him power over all flesh, that he should give eternal life to as many as thou hast given him. And this is life eternal, that they might know thee the only true God, and Jesus Christ, whom thou hast sent. I have glorified thee on the earth: I have finished the work which thou gavest me to do. And now, O Father, glorify thou me with thine own self with the glory which

I had with thee before the world was." (Jn 17:1-5)

Joined with God by the Spirit

I know I am using a lot of scripture, but these things are important to comprehend and my words mean nothing. I am just a humble servant of God, but it is God's words that bring understanding and conviction and eternal life not mine. Besides that, some people reading this material may not have access to a Bible. The fact is we are gifts from the Father to the Son, handpicked and prepared to be harvested. Once we are ready the Father gives us to Jesus who has provided the sacrifice for sin which in turn opens the door to salvation. Jesus declares over and over again in these verses that those whom God gave Him, He will give eternal life and no-one can take them away from Him. We all have the same Holy Spirit living in us because God prepared us for salvation and then He gave us to His Son Jesus, who paid the price for our salvation. Then the Father provided us with the Holy Spirit who abides in the Father, the Son and in the believer making them all one. No one can take the Holy Spirit away from the Father. No one can take the Holy Spirit way from the Son and no one can take the Holy Spirit away from anyone who has been born of the Spirit.

When I was growing up the most valuable things that I had were the things that my father had given me. Even though I don't think I ever heard him say that he loved me until I was grown, I knew it in my heart. When he passed into eternity there was not much inheritance because my parents never had a lot. Funny thing though, I never knew we were poor when I was a child. Everybody I knew lived the same way that we did. I'm glad it was that way, never-the-less, the few things that I did get from my dad, I still have and no-one will take those things from me. I believe this is how Jesus feels about us, we are gifts from His Father and no-one will ever take us from Him. This is how Jesus, the Son of God, protects our salvation. He will never lose us, cast us out, or let anyone take us away from Him.

Chapter Twelve

Perfect Love Casteth Out Fear

We are the Part of God that Man Can See

I told you earlier that when Jesus was here He was the manifestation of God, in other words, He was the part of God that mankind could see. He was the method that God the Father used to make Himself known to man. Now that He is gone, we (Christians), are the part of God that mankind can see. When people look at you do they have a reason to glorify God because of the work that He has done in your life? Once again, I have made it clear that once you are saved no-one can take your salvation away because just as all three parts of God were involved in your salvation, so are all three parts of God involved in keeping your salvation. Now that we understand that

God lives in us it takes us to the next level, because if we have God in us, then we also have the love of God in us. With this in mind, I want to tell you some things about the love of God that lives inside the Christian which should be life-changing.

> *"Beloved, let us love one another: for love is of God; and every one that loveth is born of God, and knoweth God. He that loveth not knoweth not God; for God is love. In this was manifested the love of God toward us, because that God sent his only begotten Son into the world, that we might live through him. Herein is love, not that we loved God, but that he loved us, and sent his Son to be the propitiation for our sins. Beloved, if God so loved us, we ought also to love one another. No man hath seen God at any time. If we love one another, God dwelleth in us, and his love is perfected in us. Hereby know we that we dwell in him, and he in us, because he hath given us of his Spirit. And we have seen and do testify that the Father sent the Son to be the Saviour of the world. Whosoever shall confess that Jesus is the Son of God, God dwelleth in him, and he in God. And we have known and believed the love that God hath to us. God is love; and he that dwelleth in love dwelleth in God, and God in him. Herein is our love made perfect, that we may have boldness in the day of judgment: because as he is, so are we in this world. There is no fear in love; but perfect love casteth out fear: because fear*

hath torment. He that feareth is not made perfect in love. We love him, because he first loved us." (Jn 4:7-19)

Now that Jesus has ascended into heaven and is seated at the right hand of God the Father, Christians are the only part of God that mankind can see here on earth today. When people look at you do they have a reason to glorify God because of the work that He has done in your life? The Bible teaches that mankind was created to bring glory to God. (Is 43:7) This means we should give, and encourage others to give, God worshipful praise, honor, distinction and thanksgiving. If you have the Spirit of God within you, then you should also have the love of God in you. If you have the love of God, then you should no longer have the fear of eternal punishment.

Perfect Love Casteth Out Fear

In the verses used above, we can also see that our salvation is secure because perfect love casteth out fear, verse 18. If you are born of the Spirit of God, then you have perfect love because God is love and He lives inside of you. In the following verses, talking to those who have not been born of the Spirit, Jesus told us that the one that people should fear the most is God the Father because He has the authority to destroy both the soul and the body. Since the definition of death is the separation of the spirit from the body and man has three parts just like God does, then this verse is logical. In this scenario the spirit of the man (not the Holy Spirit) has departed from the body, the spirit is the part that provides the breath of life. The soul and the body still remain and the soul and the body will never die (the worm dieth not) but they will be destined to suffer in hell for eternity. This body that we have now will perish, but the saved will receive a glorified body and the lost will also have a body in hell.

> *"And fear not them which kill the body, but are not able to kill the soul: but rather fear him which is able to destroy both soul and body in hell." (Matt 10:28)*

> *"And I say unto you my friends, Be not afraid of them that kill the body, and after that have no more that they can do. But I will forewarn you whom ye shall fear: Fear him, which after he hath killed hath power to cast into hell; yea, I say unto you, Fear him. " (Lk 12:4-5)*

But Jesus goes on to say, fear not, because to God, His children are extremely important, even to the point that every hair on your head is numbered. He concludes by explaining that the children of God are those who believe in Christ as their savior and confess Him before men.

> *"Are not five sparrows sold for two farthings, and not one of them is forgotten before God? But even the very hairs of your*

head are all numbered. Fear not therefore: ye are of more value than many sparrows. Also I say unto you, Whosoever shall confess me before men, him shall the Son of man also confess before the angels of God: But he that denieth me before men shall be denied before the angels of God." (Lk 12:6-9)

"Are not two sparrows sold for a farthing? and one of them shall not fall on the ground without your Father. But the very hairs of your head are all numbered. Fear ye not therefore, ye are of more value than many sparrows. Whosoever therefore shall confess me before men, him will I confess also before my Father which is in heaven. But whosoever shall deny me before men, him will I also deny before my Father which is in heaven." (Matt 10:29-33)

If You Are Saved the Devil is Already Defeated

Some people believe these passages are referring to the devil, but I believe it is clearly talking about God the Father. After that you are saved you have already defeated the devil concerning the battle over your soul, but you have also been given the power of the Holy Spirit to overcome him and therefore there is no more need to fear him. As we have seen in I Cor 15:51-58, Jesus has already defeated the devil over death and the grave and He has given this gift to all who believe and therefore there is nothing left to fear. I believe however, Jesus is talking about the fear of God here and not the devil because the devil does not have the power or authority to cast anyone into hell. In fact he, the devil, will be cast into the lake of fire himself at the end. As it is pointed out in these verses, if you accept Christ as your savior you are a child of God and God loves His children. Those who reject Christ should fear God and the fact that God will cast them into hell when they leave this life. Those who accept Christ will be professed by Christ as the children of God and so they no longer need to fear Him. So now I will make my point; If our greatest fear as humans should be God because he has the power to destroy our body and soul in hell and allow our sins to condemn us for eternity, but we already have victory over the devil, death, hell and the grave and are now God's children, then we should no longer have this fear. If it were possible however, that this salvation that we cling to can be lost, or taken away, then that fear would return. If I am concerned that my salvation can be lost I still live in fear. Fortunately, Christians can live without fear of what the devil or God can do to us because no-one can take away our salvation, not the devil, not Jesus, not the Father or even we ourselves. If this were not true then salvation would mean nothing because we could have it today and lose it tomorrow and fear would remain the whole time. Christians should now only fear God in the way they fear their earthly fathers. They live righteous lives because they fear disappointing God only, not because they fear destruction of the body or the soul. My body and soul Is precious to God, so much so, that the hairs of my head are all numbered by Him. I will profess Him before man boldly that I might be professed to God by Christ when the time comes.

> *"Wherefore I put thee in remembrance that thou stir up the gift of God, which is in thee by the putting on of my hands. For God hath not given us the spirit of fear; but of power, and of love, and of a sound mind." (2Tim 1:6-7)*

> *"Honour all men. Love the brotherhood. Fear God. Honour the king." (1Pet 2:17)*

Perfect love does cast out all fear, fear of God and the devil. Perfect love also cast out the fear of what man can do to you. Love cast out fear of natural disasters, the fear of starvation the fear of destruction and harm. Those who love God and trust Him have nothing to fear accept their own failure to keep God first. "The fear of the Lord is the beginning of wisdom." (Pr 9:10) This is true because without the fear of the Lord we would not seek God and would never know the amazing love of God that can set us free from fear.

Chapter Thirteen

The Holy Spirit

The Significance of the Holy Spirit

When I first starting writing this book, I didn't feel it was necessary to spend a lot of time talking about the ministry of the Holy Spirit. Since then, I have found that many religious organizations, some of whom consider themselves to be Christian, deny the existence and ministry of the Holy Spirit. Considering the significance of His existence and ministry, I feel the Spirit has led me to include an entire chapter in this book dedicated to His ministry.

The Holy Spirit is the power of God that makes Christ one with the Father and makes us one with Christ. Jesus was not only one with the Father, but also one with the Holy Spirit. It is the indwelling or sharing of the Spirit that makes Jesus one with the Father and it is the indwelling of the spirit in the Christian that makes them one with Christ and the Father. Just prior to the crucifixion of Christ, He revealed to His Apostles that the Spirit was with them at that time, but there would soon come a time when the Spirit would be in them.

> *"Even the spirit of truth; whom the world cannot receive, because it seeth him not, neither knoweth him: but ye know him; for he dwelleth with you, and shall be in you."*
> *(Jn 14:17)*

The Spirit Shall be in You

In this verse Jesus tells the Apostles that the Spirit of God cannot be seen and because the world can't see Him they don't know Him. Then He tells them, but you know Him because He is living with you right now. It was Jesus who was living or dwelling with them at that time, so He was referring to the Spirit within Himself. Jesus was one with the Spirit. I guess you could say, since Jesus is the manifestation of God, and the Spirit is the Spirit of God, then Jesus was also the manifestation of the Spirit. The Apostles could not see the Spirit, but they could know Him because He was dwelling with them in the person of Jesus Christ. Then Jesus told them that the Spirit would soon be living or dwelling in them. The Holy Spirit did not indwell the believers until after Jesus died, was buried, resurrected and ascended into heaven. After

His ascension, then the Spirit was sent to indwell the believers. Now look at verse eighteen:

> *"I will not leave you comfortless; I will come to you." (Jn 14:18*

Jesus and the Holy Spirit are One

We know that after Jesus ascended He did not come back to earth in a body again. Yet, here He tells the Apostles that He would not leave them comfortless. What He is telling them is that He and the Holy Spirit, which He is calling a comforter, are one. Jesus did not come back, but He did not leave them alone either. He did not come back in the flesh, but He did come back in the Spirit because the Holy Spirit whom He sent back to indwell the believer is God. Notice in the verse He says "I will come". Jesus is the body of God and the Holy Spirit is the Spirit of God, but they are both part of the same God. Still, Jesus is not finished trying to explain this so look at the next verse:

> *"Yet a little while, and the world seeth me no more; but ye see me: because I live, ye shall live also." (Jn 14:19)*

In this verse Jesus tells them that soon He would no longer be on earth in the flesh and therefore the world would no longer believe in His existence, but because of the indwelling of the Holy Spirit the

Apostles would still know Him because He would still be with them. We know this is what He meant because of the rest of the verse. "because I live" He was referring to the Spiritual life that is provided to Him through the Holy Spirit. "ye shall live also", They had not yet received the Spiritual life that they had been promised because they had not received the Holy Spirit yet, but Jesus tells them here that they will soon possess Spiritual life just like He did. Next is the quencher statement that we have been working towards:

> "At that day ye shall know that I am in my Father, and ye in me, and I in you." (Jn 14:20)

This verse sums it all up. He tells them that you do not have complete understanding of what I am telling you right now because you have not been indwelt by the Holy Spirit yet, but soon you will be. Once you have received the Spirit you will know immediately that something is different. You will have Spiritual life, you will have the power of God living inside you, and you will have spiritual understanding. You will then be one with God the Father and God the Son and God the Holy Spirit by the indwelling of the Spirit of God because if you have one part of God, then you have all of God because they are all one God, and now you are one with them. Does that mean that once we get saved that we become deity also with God. Not exactly, we do have God living inside us through the indwelling of the Spirit, but unlike God, we also have a sinful body that we haven't shed yet. God is not capable of sin, and as long as we are, then we cannot be considered equal with God, but one day we will shed this sinful body. In the Spiritual realm we will be the same as Christ because we will be like Him, but there is still a chain of command and God will still be head over all.

> *"Beloved, now are we the sons of God, and it doth not yet appear what we shall be; but we know that, when he shall appear, we shall be like him; for we shall see him as he is." (1Jn 3:2)*

The Holy Spirit is the Seal

I believe these scriptures prove that the Holy Spirit does exist, and not only does He exist, but He is equal to God because He is God and He is Jesus. He is just a part of God that cannot be seen just as the Father is also a spirit that cannot be seen. So, why is this important as it relates to the fact that a saved person cannot lose their salvation? Glad you asked; actually there are several reasons why this is important to comprehend. First, the Holy Spirit is called the seal of our salvation. In Jesus' time the Roman Empire ruled over the areas where Jesus lived and where He ministered. Whenever important documents were brought for the king's signature he would place his seal on the document. The king's seal was unique from anyone else's and his seal could not be broken by anyone without the king's permission. The seal was formed on the document, or whatever was being sealed, by pouring wax on it and then the king would press his emblem into the wax. The punishment for breaking the king's seal was death. This same type of seal was placed on Jesus tomb. (Matt 27:65-66) The Bible says that our salvation is secured by the seal of the Holy Spirit. In other words, the Holy Spirit is responsible for keeping our salvation secure. Of course, who could be better qualified or positioned for the job, since it is the indwelling of the Holy Spirit that gives us eternal life to begin with then it is also the Holy Spirit's job to ensure that we can't lose that life. Jesus told the Apostles, I live and when you receive the Spirit then you will live also. (Jn 14:19) They were already alive when Jesus told them that so therefore He was obviously talking about Spiritual life which comes from the indwelling of the Spirit. It is the Spirit that gives us Spiritual life and it is the Spirit that seals that spiritual life. This is the seal of God, the seal of the Spirit of God and the seal of the King of Kings and the Lord of Lords, Jesus Christ. There are numerous verses that refer to the seal of the Spirit. I will not quote them all here, but I can share some of them with you.

> *"And grieve not the Holy Spirit of God, whereby ye are sealed unto the day of redemption." (Eph 4:30)*

Additional references: Eph 1:13-14, 2Cor 1:21-22, Jn 6:27

The Earnest of the Spirit

The Holy Spirit is the earnest or down payment of our salvation. He is God's promise or guarantee that we will receive an eternal inheritance. I believe just about everyone has been in a situation at one time or another when they were required to provide earnest money. This is a common practice in our society today. Earnest money is a down payment that you make on a purchase which is a promise by the buyer that he will follow through with everything that he has promised. The indwelling of the Holy Spirit is called the earnest, or down payment, or deposit that God gave us as a guarantee that everything that He has promised us concerning everlasting life and all the glory of heaven and all the promises that God makes to His believers in the Bible will be fulfilled. God is not a man that He could break His promises. (Num 23:19)

> *"In whom ye also trusted, after that ye heard the word of truth, the gospel of your salvation: in whom also after that ye believed, ye were sealed with that Holy Spirit of promise, Which is the earnest of our inheritance until the redemption of the purchased possession, unto the praise of his glory" (Eph 1:13-14)*

The Holy Spirit is the promise of God concerning our inheritance (all the things we are entitled to as the children of God) until the time comes when our redemption is completed which will be at the rapture or the resurrection. The children of God (the believers) are the purchased possession.

The Spirit of Adoption

The Holy Spirit is called the Spirit of adoption and is the part of God that bears witness together with our spirits that we are the children of God by being adopted into God's family by the authority of the Holy Spirit. Take a look at these verses below that declare to the believer that we are adopted into God's family and are now entitled to the inheritance of God through the indwelling of the Holy Spirit.

> *"For as many as are led by the Spirit of God, they are the sons of God. For ye have not received the spirit of bondage again to fear; but ye have received the Spirit of adoption, whereby we cry Abba, Father: The Spirit itself beareth witness with our spirit, that we are the children of God: And if children, then heirs; heirs of God, and joint heirs with Christ; if so be that we suffer with him, that we may be also glorified together." (Rom 8:14-17)*

The Holy Spirit is the Source of Our Resurrections

The Holy Spirit is the one who will raise you up from the dead. The Bible teaches that it is the Spirit that gives eternal spiritual life and therefore it is the Spirit that rose up Jesus Christ and it will be the Holy Spirit that lives inside of you that will also raise you up from the grave when the time comes.

> *"But the Spirit of him that raised up Jesus from the dead dwell in you, he that raised up Christ from the dead shall also quicken your mortal bodies by his Spirit that dwelleth in you." (Rom 8:11)*

To quicken means to give life, I could go on and on about the Holy Spirit and His ministry, but I believe you get the idea. The Holy Spirit is the comforter, The Holy Spirit is our Spiritual guide, the Holy Spirit gives us eternal life, the Holy Spirit makes us the sons of God, the Holy Spirit makes us the temple of the almighty living God, the Holy Spirit provides us with immediate access to God the Father and the Son, the Holy Spirit entitles us to the inheritance we are guaranteed, the Holy Spirit convicts us and leads us to God, it will be the power of the Holy Spirit that raises us up from the dead. Do not underestimate the power or the ministry of the Holy Spirit. To deny or reject the Holy Spirit is to deny the power of God.

Jesus said the only sin that cannot be forgiven is to speak out against the Holy Spirit:

> *"Wherefore I say unto you, all manner of sin and blasphemy shall be forgiven unto men: but the blasphemy against the Holy Ghost shall not be forgiven unto men. And whosoever speaketh a word against the Son of man, it shall be forgiven him: but whosoever speaketh against the Holy Ghost, it shall not be forgiven him, neither in this world, neither in the world to come." (Matt 12:31-32)*

It shocks me that so many religious people who claim to know God and claim to be Christians, continue to deny the existence and ministry of the Holy Spirit. The Holy Spirit is God and it is the Holy Spirit that makes us the children of God and it is the Holy Spirit that will raise us from the dead.

Chapter Fourteen

The Rapture

Our Salvation Occurs When We Accept Christ

We should know that our salvation is secured for all eternity because it is referred to as something that has already happened at the time we were saved, not something that we are waiting to happen when we die. This is evident by the event in the Bible called the rapture. You will not find the word "Rapture" in the Bible. This word means to be caught up. The phrase is found in First Thessalonians 4:17:

> *"Then we which are alive and remain shall be caught up together with them in the clouds, to meet the Lord in the air: and so shall we ever be with the Lord." (1Thes 4:17)*

The scripture here is describing the day when Jesus returns to claim what is His (Christians). The rapture is when Jesus returns to retrieve the born again. Those whose spirits have already separated from their physical bodies at that time are described as being asleep in Christ. When you die, if you are saved, then your spirit is immediately in the presence of God, however your body is in the grave.

> *"Now he that hath wrought us for the selfsame thing is God, who also hath given unto us the earnest of the Spirit. Therefore we are always confident, knowing that, whilst we are at home in the body, we are absent from the Lord: (For we walk by faith, not by sight:) We are confident, I say, and willing rather to be absent from the body, and to be present with the Lord. (2Cor 5:5-8)*

Christians Who Have Passed are Asleep.

The scripture doesn't use the term death here because Christians are never separated from God when they separate from their bodies, but their bodies will be asleep until the rapture takes place and then they will be rejoined. Anyhow, it says that those who are asleep, also referred to as the dead in Christ, will rise out of the graves first with their heavenly bodies, and then those who are saved, but still living, will be changed. Our corrupt bodies must put on incorruption and our mortal bodies must put on immortality. (Then we will understand Jesus because we will be like Him.) We will receive our heavenly bodies at that time, and then we will be caught up (raptured) together with the Lord in the air as Jesus escorts us to our eternal home.

> *"But I would not have you to be ignorant, brethren, concerning them which are asleep, that ye sorrow not, even as others which have no hope. For if we believe that Jesus died and rose again, even so them also which sleep in Jesus will God bring with him. For this we say unto you by the word of the Lord, that we which are alive and remain unto the coming of the Lord shall not prevent them which are asleep. For the Lord himself shall descend from heaven with a shout, with the voice of the archangel, and with the trump of God: and the dead in Christ shall rise first: Then we which are alive and remain shall be caught up together with them in the clouds, to meet the Lord in the air: and so shall we ever be with the Lord. Wherefore comfort one another with these words." (1Thes 4:13-18)*

Additional References: I Cor 15:51-58

Eternal Life Begins at the Time of Our Salvation

If those believers who have already died before Christ comes will be retrieved from the grave, then it is obvious that they were saved before they died and it has nothing to do with anything they did before they died other than accepting Christ. Therefore it should also be obvious that eternal life begins at the time of our salvation. We will not have our eternal bodies until the rapture takes place, but we already have our eternal life because our spirits are never separated from God and our bodies are only asleep until they are glorified and rejoined with our spirits. The fact that our eternal life begins at the time of our salvation is evident by the language used to describe the salvation experience.

> *"If I have told you earthly things, and ye believe not, how shall ye believe, if I tell you of heavenly things? And no man hath ascended up to heaven, but he that came down from heaven, even the Son of man which is in heaven. And as Moses lifted up the serpent in the wilderness, even so must the Son of man be lifted up: That whosoever believeth in him should not perish, but have eternal life. For God so loved the world, that he gave his only begotten Son, that whosoever believeth in him should not perish, but have life. For God sent not his Son into the world to condemn the world; but that the world through him might be saved. He that believeth on him is not condemned: but he that believeth not is condemned already, because he hath not believed in the name of the only begotten Son of God." (Jn 3:12-18)*

Two different times in these few verses Jesus declares that whoever believes in Him has eternal life. He is not referring to something that they will have sometime in the future. Your first birth gave you temporal worldly life; your second birth gave you everlasting spiritual life. When you are saved the Spirit of God dwells in you, He becomes one with you and therefore you immediately receive eternal life through God's Spirit. In verse fifteen above, Jesus declares that whoever believes will never perish, but they **HAVE,** not will have, eternal life. This is the Greek word "Ekho", (exos eeho), which when used in this tense means that you now possess, hold or you are possessed with. Therefore from the moment that you are saved you hold or are possessed with eternal life through the Spirit of God. In verse sixteen, He reiterates the point and clearly says whoever believes is not condemned, but already possesses eternal life, and in verse eighteen, again He stresses that if you don't believe, you are already condemned because you do not possess the Holy Spirit. This fact is out of your hands, either you believe and you possess the Holy Spirit, or you do not believe and you do not possess the Holy Spirit. If you could lose your salvation, then you would make this a false statement because you cannot be unborn of the Spirit. Once your spirit is joined, or united, or becomes one with the Spirit of God, they cannot be separated. Every place where the scriptures describes salvation it uses this language which indicates that this is something that happens immediately when you are saved and is eternal in nature.

Not Possible for Christians to be Demon Possessed

On a side note, this might be a good time to tell you that this why Christians can never be demon possessed. I'm sure most of you have probably heard this before, but never really received a good explanation of why this true. Since you, as a Christian, are indwelt by the Holy Spirit at the time of your salvation, then you might say that you are already God possessed. The scripture uses the term devil possessed when referring to the devil's spirit inside you because when the devil moves in he takes control of your body. In other words, your body is controlled by the devil at that time. The terminology used to describe a person when the Holy Spirit moves in is indwelt. That is because, unlike the devil, when the Holy Spirit lives in you, He will only control as much of your body as you surrender to Him. In addition to keeping your salvation secure He is there to guide you into righteous living, but He doesn't take control of you because if we had to live righteously, and had no choice, then there would be no glory in it. It pleases God when we make the righteous choices in our lives because we love Him. We were created for His pleasure. The child of God cannot be devil possessed because they are already possessed by the Holy Spirit and since God is light and the devil is darkness, light and darkness cannot dwell in the same place at the same time. When light moves in (the Holy Spirit), the darkness (devils and demons) are forced out. Perhaps this is one reason why Jesus put so much emphasis on casting out demons. Demons must be cast out before the Holy Spirit can move in.

The Word of God reveals this truth in a profound way. Since the devil controls this world, the world and its unsaved inhabitants are described as darkness. On the other hand, Jesus was the light that came into the world and Christians are called children of light.

> *"In the beginning was the Word, and the Word was with God, and the Word was God. The same was in the beginning with God. All things were made by him; and without him was not any thing made that was made. In him was life; and the life was the light of men. And the light shineth in darkness; and the darkness comprehended it not. There was a man sent from God, whose name was John. The same came for a witness, to bear witness of the Light, that all men through him might believe. He was not that Light, but was sent to bear witness of that Light. That was the true Light, which lighteth every man that cometh into the world. He was in the world, and the world was made by him, and the world knew him not. He came unto his own, and his own received him not. But as many as received him, to them gave he power to become the sons of God, even to them that believe on his name:"*
> *(Jn 1:1-12)*

"This then is the message which we have heard of him, and declare unto you, that God is light, and in him is no darkness at all. If we say that we have fellowship with him, and walk in darkness, we lie, and do not the truth:" (1Jn 1:5-6)

Light and darkness cannot reside in the same place. Where light exist there is no darkness and when light is revealed darkness flees.

"Then Jesus said unto them, Yet a little while is the light with you. Walk while ye have the light, lest darkness come upon you: for he that walketh in darkness knoweth not whither he goeth. While ye have light, believe in the light, that ye may be the children of light. These things spake Jesus, and departed, and did hide himself from them." (Jn 12:35)

"For yourselves know perfectly that the day of the Lord so cometh as a thief in the night. For when they shall say, Peace and safety; then sudden destruction cometh upon them, as travail upon a woman with child; and they shall not escape. But ye, brethren, are not in darkness, that that day should overtake you as a thief. Ye are all the children of light, and the children of the day: we are not of the night, nor of darkness. Therefore let us not sleep, as do others; but let us watch and be sober. For they that sleep sleep in the night; and they that be drunken are drunken in the night. But let

> *us, who are of the day, be sober, putting on the breastplate of faith and love; and for an helmet, the hope of salvation." (1Thes 5:2-8)*

We are Children of Light

Jesus was the light of the world while He was here and He made it clear to the Apostles, even though they probably didn't understand what He was saying, that they needed to accept the light while He was here or they would lose their opportunity. Jesus was the light because the Holy Spirit of God was in Him and that is how and why He was and is one with the Father. If they accepted Christ while He was here, then He would send the light (The Holy Spirit) to them when He left and that is just what He did.

So to sum it up, we are saved for eternity, without the possibility of losing our salvation because once we accepted Christ as our savior we received the light of God in us through the Holy Spirit and once you have the light in you it never leaves. Whether you live until the rapture takes place, or you die a physical death and your body goes to the grave and your soul to heaven before the rapture is irrelevant, because you are already saved at the time that you believed and accepted Jesus and that will never change.

Chapter Fifteen

Great Joy in Heaven

The Joy of a Saved Soul

I believe our salvation is secured for all eternity because there is great joy in heaven over one sinner that repents.

> *"I say unto you, that likewise joy shall be in heaven over one sinner that repenteth, more than over ninety and nine just persons, which need no repentance." (Lk 15:7)*

In the book of Luke chapter fifteen Jesus tells three parables describing what it is like when a lost person comes to God and is saved. The parable of the lost sheep verses 4-7, the parable of the lost coin verses 8-10 and the parable of the lost son verses 11-32. These parables were told to the scribes and Pharisees by Jesus in order for Him to explain why He spent most of His time with sinners rather than with those who considered themselves to be righteous. Regardless, there are a number of things we can learn from these parables. In each parable the lost item appears to have been something or someone who had previously belonged to the owner, but the owner had lost them. Some would tell you that this proves that a person can lose their salvation. Since there are so many other reasons that I have already revealed to you why that is not possible, let me explain what Jesus was teaching in these parables. In the case of the lost son, we can assume that the father and the son had a good relationship at one time. Small children are protected from their sins until they reach the age of reason or accountability. (1Jn 2:12) We already know this. Once the son in this story reached the age that he could decide whether or not to accept his father's rules and continue to abide under his protection or not, the younger son chose to reject his father's plan for his life and went out on his own. The end result was destruction and eventually he came to his senses and came back to his father. Jesus was using a story that almost everyone with children can relate to. We are all close to our children when they are small, but once they grow up they can hardly wait to get out from under their parents control. To tell the truth, most of the time, the parents are ready for them to leave by this time as well because of their rebellion. You would not believe the number of times I have heard women say that they got married because they couldn't wait to get out from under their parent's control. It is well documented and understood also, how teenage boys almost exclusively have conflict with their fathers and can't wait to move out. In recent years more and more of these rebellious teenagers are coming back home sooner because they can't survive on their own any more. This is another topic for another time. The point is there is conflict there and they would leave if they had a choice.

Age of Accountability

All people from the time of their birth, belong to God until they reach an age that they are able to understand God's plan for their lives (age of accountability), and then they either accept God's direction, or they choose to reject it. Some accept right away, some wonder off for a while, but then after they have seen the world and what it has to offer they eventually come back to God and accept His offer. Some never do decide to come back and they choose what the world has to offer instead. The significance of this story, for my purpose here, is the fact that there is much rejoicing in heaven before God and the angels over a lost son who decides to come back to God. Now let us look at the story:

> *"Likewise, I say unto you, there is joy in the presence of the angels of God over one sinner that repenteth." (Lk 15:10)*

"And the son said unto him, Father, I have sinned against heaven, and in thy sight, and am no more worthy to be called thy son. But the father said to his servants, Bring forth the best robe, and put it on him; and put a ring on his hand, and shoes on his feet: And bring hither the fatted calf, and kill it; and let us eat, and be merry: For this my son was dead, and is alive again; he was lost, and is found. And they began to be merry. Now his elder son was in the field: and as he came and drew nigh to the house, he heard musick and dancing. And he called one of the servants, and asked what these things meant. And he said unto him, Thy brother is come; and thy father hath killed the fatted calf, because he hath received him safe and sound. And he was angry, and would not go in: therefore came his father out, and intreated him. And he answering said to his father, Lo, these many years do I serve thee, neither transgressed I at any time thy commandment: and yet thou never gavest me a kid, that I might make merry with my friends: But as soon as this thy son was come, which hath devoured thy living with harlots, thou hast killed for him the fatted calf. And he said unto him, Son, thou art ever with me, and all that I have is thine. It was meet that we should make merry, and be glad: for this thy brother was dead, and is alive again; and was lost, and is found." (Lk 15:21-32)

A Reason to Rejoice

If God is Omniscient, (All knowing), He knows the past, present and future, why would there be rejoicing in heaven over a sinner that repents and gets saved if in just a short matter of time he could lose his salvation and be lost again. If salvation is not secured forever there is little to rejoice about. The reason there is rejoicing in heaven over one sinner that repenteth unto salvation is because our salvation is kept by God the Father, God the Son and God the Holy Spirit and not at all dependent upon the child of God's ability to live without sinning. **GLORY BE TO GOD!** I've said it before, and I will say it again here, we do not earn our salvation by being a good person or doing good works. We are saved by the grace of God through the redeeming work of our savior and Lord Jesus Christ and absolutely nothing that we ourselves did other than believe God's word and accept it as the truth. We did not earn our salvation and we are not capable of being a good enough person to stay saved if that were what it required. When we decide to repent and turn from the way that we have chosen to go, and go back to the Father like the young man in the story did, then we are reconciled to God the Father just like he was reconciled to his father. In this story we also see the reaction of other children of God concerning the younger brother's reconciliation. The older brother was angry that the father forgave the younger brother. The father in turn explains to the older brother that it is right that they should celebrate because the younger brother was lost and now is found. Just to clarify the meaning of the story, the father also proclaims that the younger brother was dead and is now alive again. When you reach the age of accountability and choose to rebel against God, you lose your covering that is provided for Jesus' name sake, and that is when you are dead spiritually in the eyes of God. Once you realize your mistake and recognize the truth and turn from your own way back to God, then you are born of the Spirit and you can never lose it again. The older brother should have been happy and excited that his younger brother came back home, but instead he felt as though the younger brother was getting something that he didn't deserve after he had taken all that he was entitled to before he left the first time. Often Christians feel the same way when a person that they have known to be a terrible sinner their entire lives gets saved on their death bed. This entitles them to the same heaven that the person who was saved at a young age and served God all his life is entitled to. Of course there will be a difference in the rewards that they receive, but still, do they really deserve to go to heaven after they squandered their whole life serving Satan. The answer is absolutely yes, praise God that they found the fire escape just before it was too late. I think the angels in heaven and even God would celebrate the salvation of this person more than the person who had been saved all along. This person was on the verge of eternal punishment and was rescued at the last minute. A resounding yes, we should celebrate his salvation. Also consider this; this person does not deserve salvation, but salvation is not something we get because we deserve it. There is not a single person that has ever lived, or that is living now, that deserves salvation. If there was, then salvation would be something that we could earn on our own and we would not have needed a savior. The father in the story shows us what the attitude of our heavenly Father is when someone repents. That is, He is excited when someone gets saved, especially when they were lost and now they are found. When they were dead and now are alive. Yes the rejoicing over a soul being saved by God the father and the angels is proof that our salvation is safe in the hands of God and doesn't depend on us.

Perhaps the reason some Christians do not rejoice when this happens is because they do not see it the same way that God and the angels do. Look at it like this, let us say that there was a young child swimming at the river in the local swimming hole with her family and you were there with your family enjoying the sunshine and the water with this other family. While you were all there having a good time, something happen and the young child in the other family got in trouble in the water and started to drown. The father of the young child dove in and saved the young child just before it was too late. Everyone that was there and saw what happened would be rejoicing with the father that the young child was saved. It wouldn't matter if this child was always bad or always good. It would only matter that a life was saved. This is how God sees one of His children that has gone astray and is about to drift off into eternity without the light of God's Spirit inside them. I say again, yes there would be much rejoicing. But the rejoicing is because the person is saved from hell and the lake of fire for all eternity. If the young child was saved for a few minutes and then got in trouble again and drowned, there would be no rejoicing. God and the angels are rejoicing because they already know the future and when a person accepts Christ they are saved for eternity not just until they make a mistake and end up in the same condition again. If the father made every attempt to save the child, threw everything he had out to him, swam out as far as he could, did everything he could possibly do and the child still drowned, how much rejoicing would be going on then? Since God knows the future this would be the same thing. He would know that even though he may have saved the child temporarily, He was going to lose him anyhow, and then there would be no rejoicing. Our salvation is safe and secure in the hands of God.

Chapter Sixteen

The Lamb of God

Foreshadow of Things to Come

Many of the events that took place in the Old Testament foreshadowed the things that were to happen in the New Testament in order to prepare the world for the coming of Jesus Christ. Most people have heard the story of how God delivered His chosen people, the Israelites, out of bondage under the Egyptians. It was accomplished by God sending plagues to the Egyptians. Despite all of the plagues that God sent in the beginning the Egyptians continued to refuse to release God's people. These plagues represented all of the warnings that God has given to the world through the prophets about the coming savior and yet they still refused to accept Christ when He came and many still refuse Him today. In the book of Exodus you can read about the nine plagues that God sent as a warning; the plague of blood, (Ex 7:20-25), the plague of frogs, (Ex 8:1-7), the plague of lice, (Ex 8:16-19), the plague of flies, (Ex 8:20-24), the plague of the cattle, (Ex 9:1-7), the plague of boils, (Ex 8:8-12), the plague of hail, (Ex 9:13-28), the plague of locusts, (Ex 10:12-20), and the plague of darkness, (Ex 10:21-29). Despite all of these warnings the Pharaoh of Egypt still refused to let God's people go. You would think this would have been enough to convince anybody, but in the New Testament Paul the Apostle explains that God had hardened Pharaoh's heart so that the entire world could see the power of God. The Jews refused to accept Christ for the same reason. It was part of God's plan to bring salvation to the entire world by the rejection of Christ by the Israelites. God hardened the hearts of the Israelites so that salvation could be made available to all who would believe Jews and Gentiles alike.

> *"And he hardened Pharaoh's heart, that he hearkened not unto them; as the LORD had said. And the LORD said unto Moses, Pharaoh's heart is hardened, he refuseth to let the people go." (Ex 7:13-14)*

> *"For he saith to Moses, I will have mercy on whom I will have mercy, and I will have compassion on whom I will have compassion. So then it is not of him that willeth, nor of him that runneth, but of God that sheweth mercy. For the scripture saith unto Pharaoh, Even for this same*

> *purpose have I raised thee up, that I might shew my power in thee, and that my name might be declared throughout all the earth. Therefore hath he mercy on whom he will have mercy, and whom he will he hardeneth. Thou wilt say then unto me, Why doth he yet find fault? For who hath resisted his will? Nay but, O man, who art thou that repliest against God? Shall the thing formed say to him that formed it, Why hast thou made me thus? Hath not the potter power over the clay, of the same lump to make one vessel unto honour, and another unto dishonour?"*
> *(Rom 9:15-21)*

The final plague that God sent was the death of all the first born males of every household in all the land of Egypt, but the first born of Israel would be saved by the blood of the sacrificial lamb. The lamb was to be slain and the blood of the lamb was to be smeared on the side post and on the top of the door ways in all the houses were the Israelites dwelt. This blood was to provide a covering over the people in the house so that when God passed over He would not see the sins of the first born in those houses (first born doesn't mean new born) and those first born in these homes would be spared from God's wrath.

> *"And the LORD spake unto Moses and Aaron in the land of Egypt saying, This month shall be unto you the beginning of months: it shall be the first month of the year to you. Speak ye unto all the congregation of*

Israel, saying, In the tenth day of this month they shall take to them every man a lamb, according to the house of their fathers, a lamb for an house: And if the household be too little for the lamb, let him and his neighbour next unto his house take it according to the number of the souls; every man according to his eating shall make your count for the lamb. Your lamb shall be without blemish, a male of the first year: ye shall take it out from the sheep, or from the goats: And ye shall keep it up until the fourteenth day of the same month: and the whole assembly of the congregation of Israel shall kill it in the evening. And they shall take of the blood, and strike it on the two side posts and on the upper door post of the houses, wherein they shall eat it. And they shall eat the flesh in that night, roast with fire, and unleavened bread; and with bitter herbs they shall eat it. Eat not of it raw, nor sodden at all with water, but roast with fire; head with his legs, and with the purtenance thereof. And ye shall let nothing of it remain until the morning; and that which remaineth of it until the morning ye shall burn with fire. And thus shall ye eat it; with your loins girded, your shoes on your feet, and your staff in your hand; and ye shall eat it in haste: it is the LORD's passover. For I will pass through the land of Egypt this night, and will smite all the firstborn in the land of Egypt, both man and beast; and against all the gods of Egypt I will execute judgment: I am the LORD. And the blood shall be to you for a token upon the houses where ye are: and when I see the blood, I will pass over you, and the plague shall not be upon you to destroy you, when I smite the land of Egypt. And this day shall be unto you for a memorial; and ye shall keep it a feast to the LORD throughout your generations; ye shall keep it a feast by an ordinance for ever." (Ex 12:1-14)

The Lord's Passover

This was the Lord's Passover, because God passed over the homes of the Israelites due to the blood of the lamb. Jesus is our sacrificial lamb whose blood was shed to provide a covering over our sins. When God looks down on the earth and all the evil that is in it, He does not see the sins of the redeemed because they are covered by the blood of the Lamb.

> *"Purge out therefore the old leaven, that ye may be a new lump, as ye are unleavened. For even Christ our passover is sacrificed for us:" (1Cor 5:7)*
>
> *"The next day John seeth Jesus coming unto him, and saith, Behold the Lamb of God, which taketh away the sin of the world." (Jn 1:29)*
>
> *"And looking upon Jesus as he walked, he saith, Behold the Lamb of God!" (Jn 1:36)*

> *"Forasmuch as ye know that ye were not redeemed with corruptible things, as silver and gold, from your vain conversation received by tradition from your fathers; But with the precious blood of Christ, as of a lamb without blemish and without spot: Who verily was foreordained before the foundation of the world, but was manifest in these last times for you," (1Pet 1:18-20)*

These verses remind me of the song "Nothing But the Blood" written by Robert Lowry in 1876, "What can wash away my sins, nothing but the blood of Jesus, What can make me whole again, nothing but the blood of Jesus"

The Passover is now celebrated by Jewish families in remembrance of what God did for them as God told them to do. As for Christians, Jesus told the church to celebrate the Lord's Supper, sometimes called the Last supper, in remembrance of Him and how that He sacrificed His own body and blood for the salvation of those who would put their faith in Him.

> *"And when the hour was come, he sat down, and the twelve apostles with him. And he said unto them, With desire I have desired to eat this passover with you before I suffer: For I say unto you, I will not any more eat thereof, until it be fulfilled in the kingdom of God. And he took the cup, and gave thanks, and said, Take this, and divide it among yourselves: For I say unto you, I will not drink of the fruit of the vine,*

until the kingdom of God shall come. And he took bread, and gave thanks, and brake it, and gave unto them, saying, This is my body which is given for you: this do in remembrance of me. Likewise also the cup after supper, saying, This cup is the new testament in my blood, which is shed for you." (Lk 22:14-20)

Jesus is the Sacrificial Lamb

It should come as no surprise that Jesus died on the cross during the preparation of the Passover which was celebrated every year at the same exact time. This was done to commemorate the covering of the sins of the Israelites in the Old Testament by the spilt blood of the sacrificial lamb. God's timing is always perfect and He made it perfectly clear that Jesus was the sacrificial lamb who had to spill His blood to cover the sins of those who believe in Him. This had been God's plan for the salvation of the world from the beginning. Jesus paid such a tremendous price for this covering one would have to be insane to think that He would pay such great a price for our eternal life, and then turn it over to us to keep it. Jesus provided our salvation and Jesus keeps our salvation. Our sins are covered by the blood of the lamb and so shall they be forever more. Because of the final sacrifice that Jesus made for the sins of the world there remaineth no more sacrifice for sins. (Heb 10:12)

> *"And from thenceforth Pilate sought to release him: but the Jews cried out, saying, If thou let this man go, thou art not Caesar's friend: whosoever maketh himself a king speaketh against Caesar. When Pilate therefore heard that saying, he brought Jesus forth, and sat down in the judgment seat in a place that is called the Pavement, but in the Hebrew, Gabbatha. And it was the preparation of the passover, and about the sixth hour: and he saith unto the Jews, Behold your King! But they cried out, Away with him, away with him, crucify him. Pilate saith unto them, Shall I crucify your King? The chief priests answered, We have no king but Caesar. Then delivered he him therefore unto them to be crucified. And they took Jesus, and led him away." (Jn 19:12-16)*

The Jewish religion still celebrates the Passover because they still hold to the old traditions and laws, but the Christians celebrate the Lord's Supper instead for the remembrance of the sacrifice that Jesus made in order to deliver all men, Jews and Gentiles alike, from their sins. Jesus is the sacrificial lamb that takes away the sins of the world to anyone who will believe.

Chapter Seventeen

Reservations in Heaven

A Place Reserved in Heaven

We are secure in our salvation because God Himself has made reservations in heaven for us. It is one thing when a person makes reservations for themselves, but when God does it for you that is a whole other thing. Oftentimes people will make reservations and have to cancel them at the last minute, but from God's perspective a reservation is the same as a promise made by Him because He already knows the future and so His plans never get changed. If God makes a reservation for you, you can be guaranteed that His plans will not change. If God has made reservations for you, then He has already made preparations for your arrival as well. Since God knows the future all reservations are final. Now look at these verses:

> *"Peter, an apostle of Jesus Christ, to the strangers scattered throughout Pontus, Galatia, Cappadocia, Asia, and Bithynia, Elect according to the foreknowledge of God the Father, through sanctification of the Spirit, unto obedience and sprinkling of the blood of Jesus Christ: Grace unto you, and peace, be multiplied. Blessed be the God and Father of our Lord Jesus Christ, which according to his abundant mercy hath begotten us again unto a lively hope by the resurrection of Jesus Christ from the dead, To an inheritance incorruptible, and undefiled, and that fadeth not away, reserved in heaven for you, Who are kept by the power of God through faith unto salvation ready to be revealed in the last time." (1Pet 1:1-5)*

> *"Henceforth there is laid up for me a crown of righteousness, which the Lord, the righteous judge, shall give me at that day: and not to me only, but unto all them also that love his appearing." (2Tim 4:8)*

In these verses we are told that not only has God already made reservations for us in heaven, but that He has already begun to prepare for our arrival by laying aside our rewards. If you have ever gone to a busy restaurant, or had to make reservations for a hotel, then you understand what that means. If you made the reservations, then it is a promise from you that you will be there at a certain day and time and you won't be late. Well, God has made that promise for you and God is not a man that He should break His promises. A reservation also gives the place where you are going an opportunity for them to prepare for your arrival. No-one will be surprised when you show up. Your table will be waiting for you, or your hotel room will be clean and ready for you to come in. Jesus told the Apostles that in His Father's house were many mansions. He said, I go to prepare a place for you and if I go to prepare a place for you I will come for you so that where I am there you may be also.

> *"Let not your heart be troubled: ye believe in God, believe also in me. In my Father's house are many mansions: if it were not so, I would have told you. I go to prepare a place for you. And if I go and prepare a place for you, I will come again, and receive you unto myself; that where I am, there ye may be also." (Jn 14:1-3)*

If You Are Saved God Has Prepared for You

Did you know that if you are saved, then you already have a mansion in heaven reserved for you? How does it feel knowing that the one and only Almighty God has already made reservations in heaven for your imminent arrival? He already knows the exact time of your arrival and has already made preparations for you in heaven. Do you really think God is concerned about whether or not you are going to show up? If there was any question as to whether you would arrive on time God would not make any reservations for you. This is not up to you.

I want to have a heart to heart talk with you about something. I'm sure that many of you are saying that you don't deserve heaven and even if you stopped being a bad person today you have already done so many bad things that there is no way God could forgive you. Before I was saved I was quite fund of the alcoholic beverages and often found myself useless to the world. I did some horrible things in my life time, especially before I was saved, but even after that, I still made some bad decisions on occasion. I went in the US Air force when I was just barely seventeen years old. I was going to bars and getting wasted with the rest of the guys at that young age. My brothers and I fought like cats and dogs. I fought with my brother John, who was one year older than me every day. At one point I swore to him that I was going to kill him when I got old enough to figure out how to get away with it. I lied, I stole, I cheated, and basically I was a child of the Devil and did all the things that people do before they know God. After I got saved my desires changed, I didn't want to live like that anymore, but it didn't all change overnight. I still allowed the devil to get to me on several occasions and I still did some things that could be considered unforgiveable. Here is the difference; before I was saved, I did everything for me and after I was saved, I started doing everything for others. Before I was saved, I committed sins knowingly and willingly and after I was saved, I made some terrible mistakes. My wife and I were watching the show "Chosen" the other day, (If you have not been watching it is a good show) and Mary had fallen back into her sinful lifestyle. Peter and Mathew went and found her and brought her back to Jesus. Mary was embarrassed and ashamed and didn't want to face Jesus. She told Jesus that she couldn't be the kind of person that she needed to be to be a Christian. Jesus told her you don't have to be. Then He asked her if she thought that she would never sin again after she was converted? He said what God wants is your heart and you already gave Him that. The rest will come in time, although maybe not here on earth. As long as we live on this earth and still have these earthly bodies we are not going to stop sinning. God created us and He knows this. Now, if Mary had not felt guilty about what she had been doing and was not at all embarrassed or ashamed, then there would be doubt as to whether she actually ever gave God her heart or not.

Becoming Christ-like

When I accepted Christ I didn't stop being David and become a different person altogether. God took me where I was and began working on me to make me more like Him, but He's still working on me and that work will not be finished until I go to heaven. I have done things in my life that I thought had rendered me useless in God's service. I am trying to change that in order to prove to myself that God can still use me. Many things will happen in your life, some you have control over and some you don't. What life as a Christian is really about is serving God. Your first obligation is to God and your second is to your fellow man. Your Christian Life is about people and how you treat them. Yes, you should stop doing certain things like lying, cheating, stealing, cursing, fornication, drunkenness etc, because these things are the things of the world not the things of God. If you are saved then eventually God will work these things out of your life a little at a time, but if you think you are going to get saved and all of sudden TADA you never sin anymore, then you are sadly mistaken. I know when I read behind other Christian authors I often feel as though I will never be as spiritual as these people are. Let me tell you a secret, no-one is without sin. "Let he who is without sin cast the first stone" (Jn 8:7). Those people are still sinners also. God can save anyone and God can use anyone that will surrender themselves enough to the Holy Spirit to allow it. Even before I was saved, for the most part, I treated people fairly well, but I did not go out of my way to help anyone. The Bible teaches that a man should work for a living, I have always believed that, but it goes on to say that the main reason you should work is so that you will have to give to those in need. WHAT, I thought I was working to provide for me and my family, not others. I used to get angry and punch holes through doors and walls, I suppose I thought this is how you act manly, but God says be angry and sin not, WHAT, that is weird. Since I have been saved I realized that this was just an intimidation tool that I had learned from the way I grew up. Everyone gets angry occasionally, that is not a sin, it is how you react to being angry that can result in sin. Yes, God wants us to change, but He doesn't expect that change to happen overnight and for some of the things that we do we may not ever be able to finish correcting it at all until the rapture. We will change some day and put all this sin behind us, in the mean time, just give God your heart and see what He can do. Following are some verses out of the Bible that deal with our manner of living after salvation.

> *"That ye put off concerning the former conversation the old man, which is corrupt according to the deceitful lusts; And be renewed in the spirit of your mind; And that ye put on the new man, which after God is created in righteousness and true holiness. Wherefore putting away lying, speak every man truth with his neighbour: for we are members one of another. Be ye angry, and sin not: let not the sun go down upon your wrath: Neither give place to the devil. Let him that stole steal no more: but rather let him labour, working with his hands the thing which is good, that he may have to give to him that needeth. Let no corrupt communication proceed out of your mouth, but that which is good to the use of edifying, that it may minister grace unto the hearers. And grieve not the holy Spirit of*

> *God, whereby ye are sealed unto the day of redemption. Let all bitterness, and wrath, and anger, and clamour, and evil speaking, be put away from you, with all malice: And be ye kind one to another, tenderhearted, forgiving one another, even as God for Christ's sake hath forgiven you." (Eph 4:22)*

This reminds me of the little children's song we used to sing to the kids on the church bus called "He's Still Working on Me" by Joel Hemphill.

He's still working on me
To make me what I ought to be
It took Him just a week to make the moon and the stars
The sun and the earth and Jupiter and Mars
How loving and patient He must be
He's still working on me.

No Sin Can Prevent Salvation

If you have not been born again, no matter what you have done in your life, there is no sin that can keep you from being saved. The only sin that cannot be forgiven is the rejection of Jesus Christ because He is your only hope. If you have been saved, then there is no sin that can cause you to lose your salvation. No matter what you have done after you were saved there is no sin that can't be forgiven and there is nothing that you can do that can make it impossible for God to use you, as long as you are remorseful and willing to ask God for forgiveness. We were all born in the flesh and the flesh has weaknesses. The devil knows what your weaknesses are. He will use those weaknesses to tempt you to sin every day. With every temptation God has provided an escape, but if your spirit is week your flesh will give in to the devil. (1 Cor 10:13) This is going to happen and there is nothing you can do to stop it, but thanks be to God, that when we do slip up and give in to the devil we are still covered by the blood of the Lamb. Give God your heart! I am so excited that God has made reservations in heaven for me and my reservations are final. My salvation is therefore safe and secure in the hands of God.

Chapter Eighteen

We are Children of Promise

Children of Promise.

The Old Testament is a record of God's old covenant between Him and father Abraham as he is often called. The New Testament is a record of God's new covenant between Him and all of mankind. Testament and covenant both mean promise. In the Greek the word "Testament" is "Diatheke", (dee'-ath'-ay'-kay) which means contract, covenant or disposition. In the Old Testament God made a promise to Abraham, the father of God's chosen people the Israelites. God made this promise to Abraham because he believed God and it was counted unto him for righteousness. (Rom 4:3)

> "For the promise, that he should be the heir of the world, was not to Abraham, or to his seed, through the law, but through the

righteousness of faith. For if they which are of the law be heirs, faith is made void, and the promise made of none effect: Because the law worketh wrath: for where no law is, there is no transgression. Therefore it is of faith, that it might be by grace; to the end the promise might be sure to all the seed; not to that only which is of the law, but to that also which is of the faith of Abraham; who is the father of us all, (As it is written, I have made thee a father of many nations,) before him whom he believed, even God, who quickeneth the dead, and calleth those things which be not as though they were. Who against hope believed in hope, that he might become the father of many nations, according to that which was spoken, So shall thy seed be. And being not weak in faith, he considered not his own body now dead, when he was about an hundred years old, neither yet the deadness of Sarah's womb: He staggered not at the promise of God through unbelief; but was strong in faith, giving glory to God; And being fully persuaded that, what he had promised, he was able also to perform. And therefore it was imputed to him for righteousness." (Rom 4:13-22)

The Old Testament Promise

You can read all about the covenant that God made with Abraham in the Book of Genesis, Chapter seventeen, verses one through ten. To sum it up however, God made a promise to Abraham because Abraham believed what God told him and he did what God told him to do. Like I said before, faith must be exercised in order for it to mean anything. Abraham believed God was who He said He was and that He would do what He said He would do and Abraham acted on that faith. This faith in God's promise to him was counted unto Abraham for righteousness. God told Abraham that in his old age (100) that he would have a son by his wife Sarah, (90) even though she was past the age of bearing children. He told him that He would be his God and that his descendents would be God's chosen people. He told him that he would bless him and his descendents and He would give them victory over their enemies and that they would inherit a land flowing with milk and honey. He told him that all the nations of the earth would be blessed through his seed. That he would multiply his seed as the stars in the heaven and as the sand on the sea shore.

Later, after Abraham and Sarah had their son Isaac, God tested Abraham's faith once more. He told Abraham to take his only son and sacrifice him to God. This was the son that God had promised to give Abraham and had promised him that all of his seed would be blessed through his son. Never-the-less Abraham took his son to the altar, believing that if God allowed him to die that he would bring him back to life so God could fulfill His promises. Now that is faith. Just before Abraham killed his son Isaac,

God stopped him and acknowledged that it was just a test and now He knew that Abraham believed Him and would do whatever He asked him to do. After that God renewed His covenant with Abraham and again promised all the things that had been promised before. (Gen 22:1-19)

The most significant promise in God's covenant with Abraham was the fact that all the nations of the earth would be blessed through his seed. Indeed, all the nations of the earth were blessed through Abraham's seed because Jesus is a descendant of Abraham. This is an important fact that most people just skip over when they read the book of Mathew. If Jesus had not been a descendent of Abraham He would not have fulfilled the promise. I told you, God had a plan from the beginning. This is one of the reasons that Jesus had to be born in the flesh here on earth because this was God's plan to provide salvation to all nations through Abraham. The New Testament is the fulfillment of the Old Testament.

Part of the covenant that God had made with Abraham included the circumcision of all his descendents and the sacrifices of animals and the shedding of blood for the remission of sins. The salvation of Israel is still to come and will be fulfilled in the Millennial reign of Christ. God has not forgotten or broken any of His promises to Israel, but what I'm telling you is just as God will complete all of the promises that He made to the Israelites under the old covenant or testament, He will also keep all of the promises or covenants that He made to those who trust in Christ according to His Word in the New Testament. The Old Testament saints will be recipients of the Old Testament promises and the Christians will be the recipients of the New Testament promises. God will keep His promises to all mankind.

> *"Brethren, my heart's desire and prayer to God for Israel is, that they might be saved. For I bear them record that they have a zeal of God, but not according to knowledge. For they being ignorant of God's righteousness, and going about to establish their own righteousness, have not submitted themselves unto the righteousness of God. For Christ is the end of the law for righteousness to every one that believeth. For Moses describeth the righteousness which is of the law, That the man which doeth those things shall live by them. But the righteousness which is of faith speaketh on this wise, Say not in thine heart, Who shall ascend into heaven? (that is, to bring Christ down from above:) Or, Who shall descend into the deep? (that is, to bring up Christ again from the dead.) But what saith it? The word is nigh thee, even in thy mouth, and in thy heart: that is, the word of faith, which we preach; That if thou shalt confess with thy mouth the Lord Jesus, and shalt believe in thine heart that God hath raised him from the dead, thou shalt be saved. For with the heart man believeth unto righteousness; and with the mouth*

confession is made unto salvation. For the scripture saith, Whosoever believeth on him shall not be ashamed. For there is no difference between the Jew and the Greek: for the same Lord over all is rich unto all that call upon him. For whosoever shall call upon the name of the Lord shall be saved." (Rom 10:1-13)

Promise to Those Who Believe in Christ

So God also made a covenant (promise) to anyone in the world that they would be offered salvation through His Son Jesus Christ if they would believe that Jesus is the Son of God and confess Him before men. This is the promise of the New Testament, or new covenant between God and man. Just as Abraham believed God and it was counted unto him for righteousness, anyone who believes in Jesus, his faith is also counted unto him for righteousness.

"For this is my blood of the new testament, which is shed for many for the remission of sins." (Matt 26:28)

"But Christ being come an high priest of good things to come, by a greater and more perfect tabernacle, not made with hands, that is to say, not of this building; Neither by the blood of goats and calves, but by his own blood he entered in once into the holy place, having obtained eternal redemption for us. For if the blood of bulls and of goats,

and the ashes of an heifer sprinkling the unclean, sanctifieth to the purifying of the flesh: How much more shall the blood of Christ, who through the eternal Spirit offered himself without spot to God, purge your conscience from dead works to serve the living God? And for this cause he is the mediator of the new testament, that by means of death, for the redemption of the transgressions that were under the first testament, they which are called might receive the promise of eternal inheritance. For where a testament is, there must also of necessity be the death of the testator. For a testament is of force after men are dead: otherwise it is of no strength at all while the testator liveth. Whereupon neither the first testament was dedicated without blood. For when Moses had spoken every precept to all the people according to the law, he took the blood of calves and of goats, with water, and scarlet wool, and hyssop, and sprinkled both the book, and all the people, Saying, This is the blood of the testament which God hath enjoined unto you." (Heb 9:11-20)

God Doesn't Break His Promises

The promise that God made to Abraham included the forgiveness of sins as did the promise God made to those who believe in Jesus. God knew that the descendents of Abraham would continue to sin and so He provided a method for those sins to be forgiven.

He also let Abraham know that even though his descendents would sin, He promised that they would be punished for their sins, but God would not break His promise with them concerning the covenant that he made. The same is true with Christians, even though God made a promise to forgive us of our sins and provide us with salvation through His Son, Jesus; He knew that we would not be able to stop sinning altogether. As with Abraham, God's children, the born again, will be punished if they commit sins, but God will not break His promise to them of eternal life through Christ.

> *"If his children forsake my law, and walk not in my judgments; If they break my statutes, and keep not my commandments; Then will I visit their transgression with the rod, and their iniquity with stripes. Nevertheless my lovingkindness will I not utterly take from him, nor suffer my faithfulness to fail. My covenant will I not break, nor alter the thing that is gone out of my lips." (Ps 89:30-34)*

God has promised us salvation through Christ and even if we sin, even if we don't deserve salvation, even if we break our promises to Him, even if we deny Christ, God will not break His promise to give us eternal life if we call upon the name of His Son Jesus Christ.

Chapter Nineteen

The Lambs Book of Life

Salvation Recorded

My salvation is secured by God for eternity because when I was saved my name was written in the Lambs Book of Life. In the Book of Revelations, which means to reveal or uncover, John the Apostle of Jesus Christ was shown a vision in which the things to come at the end times were revealed to him. There will come a day when all who ever lived on the face of the earth and have not accepted Christ as their savior, will be judged based on what they did in their lifetimes. This is called the Great White Throne Judgment. God has kept very thorough records of all the good and evil deeds of all mankind and these books will be opened at that time and all men will be judged from what is written in these books. The verses below attest to this coming judgment:

> *"And I saw a great white throne, and him that sat on it, from whose face the earth and the heaven fled away; and there was found no place for them. And I saw the dead, small and great, stand before God; and the books were opened: and another book was opened, which is the book of life: and the dead were judged out of those things which were written in the books, according to their works. And the sea gave up the dead which were in it; and death and hell delivered up the dead which were in them: and they were judged every man according to their works. And death and hell were cast into the lake of fire. This is the second death. And whosoever was not found written in the book of life was cast into the lake of fire." (Rev 20:11-15)*

The Lamb's Book of Life

When a person is born a natural birth their names are written in the book of life. When a person is born again of the Spirit, their name is written in the Lambs book of life. Of course, since to God the Father there is no past present or future, the names are already in the book from the foundation of the world. If you never accept Christ, then your name will eventually be blotted out of the book of life when you die as well. If you have accepted Christ then your name will remain in the book of life and it will be in the Lambs book of life also. Anyone whose names are not found written in the book of life shall be cast into the lake of fire. There will be a new heaven and a new earth where God will live with His people. There will also be a New Jerusalem, sometimes called the city four square, where the Lamb, (Jesus), and His bride, (the universal church, or the body of all born again believers) shall reside for eternity. No-one will be allowed to enter in the gates of the city whose names are not found in the Book of Life.

> *"He that overcometh, the same shall be clothed in white raiment; and I will not blot out his name out of the book of life, but I will confess his name before my father, and before his angels" (Rev 3:5)*

> *"And I saw a new heaven and a new earth: for the first heaven and the first earth were passed away; and there was no more sea. And I John saw the holy city, new Jerusalem, coming down from God out of heaven, prepared as a bride adorned for her husband. And I heard a great voice out of heaven saying, Behold, the tabernacle of God is with men, and he will dwell with them, and they shall be his people, and God himself shall be with them, and be their God. And God shall wipe away all tears from their eyes; and there shall be no more death, neither sorrow, nor crying, neither shall there be any more pain: for the former things are passed away. And he that sat upon the throne said, Behold, I make all things new. And he said unto me, Write: for these words are true and faithful. And*

> *he said unto me, It is done. I am Alpha and Omega, the beginning and the end. I will give unto him that is athirst of the fountain of the water of life freely. He that overcometh shall inherit all things; and I will be his God, and he shall be my son. But the fearful, and unbelieving, and the abominable, and murderers, and whoremongers, and sorcerers, and idolaters, and all liars, shall have their part in the lake which burneth with fire and brimstone: which is the second death." (Rev 21:1-8)*

Once your name has been written in the Lamb's book of life your final destination is pre-determined. God has already made reservations for you. You are covered by the blood of the Lamb. You are kept by the power of God. No-one, including yourself, is able to remove you from the Book of Life. Your name is written by Jesus in His book and you are His bride. You and Jesus are one. Your name is written in eternal ink, it is not erasable even by Jesus Himself because He cannot deny Himself. His pencil has no eraser because He knows the future before it happens, therefore in the eyes of God, if it were possible for your name to be erased it would not have been written to begin with. I know I am saved and secure in the hands of Jesus because my name is written in the Lamb's Book of life.

Chapter Twenty

The Light of the World

For the Glory of God

I believe that one of the reasons that God chose to keep our salvation safe Himself is to protect the testimony of Christians which in turn also protects God's reputation. When Jesus was here on earth in the flesh He was the light of the world. Now that He is in heaven with His Father we are tasked with being the light of the world because we are one with Jesus and God lives in us. We are now the part of God that people can see. We are the children of light.

> *"Ye are the light of the world. A city that is set on an hill cannot be hid, Neither do men light a candle, and put it under a bushel, but on a candlestick; and it giveth light unto all that are in the house. Let your light so shine before men, that they may see your good*

works, and glorify your Father which is in heaven." (Matt 5:14-16)

Additional References: Lk 12:36, Acts 26:16-18, Eph 5:8-14, I Jn 2:9-10

You should let your light shine in the world so that the world can see the light of your good works and glorify God in heaven. The great commission, which Jesus gave to his Apostles to go into the entire world and preach the gospel in order that souls might be saved, was not just for the Apostles. Each and every born again Christian has a role in this endeavor. That doesn't mean that we should all be preachers, but rather that we should all let our lights shine in the world to be a testimony for what God can do and be prepared to answer anyone concerning the hope that is in us. (I Pet 3:15)

Never too Late

Some of you may be thinking it is too late for me to be saved after the way I have lived my life, or after the things that I have done, God cannot use me to testify to others, or maybe it is too late in my life to start any kind of service for God. Remember this; Jesus was on the earth for approximately thirty years before He started His ministry and yet in just a year He was able to change the world.

I was twenty five when I accepted Christ as my savior and I have prayed and sought God's will for my life ever since then. Yet, like the children of Israel, I have wondered aimlessly in the wilderness for almost forty years before I finally realized what it is that God wants me to do. I didn't just sit around and wait for a specific calling, I have served God in many capacities since then, but I believe now I know what God wants me to do specifically. It is never too late to get saved, as long as you are still breathing and it is never too late to start a ministry for God. That is doing the specific thing that it is that God wants you to do to spread the gospel. When I was in Bible College I got a call from my family one day with the news that my grandfather was on his death bed. I wasn't sure about his relationship with God so I left school to go home and witness to him. When I got there he was in intensive care at the hospital and hooked up to a number of life support machines. At first they didn't want to let me in to see him, but God was in control and after a while they let me go in because I was family. My grandfather was a good man, but I could not recall a single word that I had ever heard him say concerning God. With that in mind I began with just the basics concerning salvation. I told him that Jesus was the Son of God and that He came here on earth in order to sacrifice Himself for the sins of men. Then I told him all you have to do is pray and ask God to forgive you for being a sinner and for Him to be your savior. Just at that moment he began to shake all over and the machines that were monitoring him began making all sorts of alarm type sounds. The intensive care nurses rushed over and asked me what I had done as they were escorting me out. On the way out I asked him if he believed and he said yes. This was an amazing moment because now, at the very last moment, I knew that my grandfather was going to heaven to be with God and there would be rejoicing in the presence of God and the angels. I have had the pleasure of God using me to lead many other people to Christ since that day, and I have rejoiced with every one of them, but I don't think non other has ever been so dear to me as then. It is never too late to be saved as long as you are breathing and it is never too late to serve God as long as you are willing.

A Good Testimony

The reason a good testimony for God is important is because all believers should have the goal of reaching lost souls for Christ. God is not willing that any should perish but that all should come to repentance (2Pet 3:9). I think this is why there is no record of anyone ever losing their salvation or anyone ever being saved more than one time. I can't believe that if something that important were true that God would leave it out of His Word. There are too many places in God's Word where it tells the stories of men being saved time and time again, and yet it never mentions anyone ever losing their salvation or having to be saved a second time. On the day of Pentecost (the day that the Apostles received the Holy Spirit) alone, it mentions the salvation of about 3000 souls.

> *"Then Peter said unto them, Repent, and be baptized every one of you in the name of Jesus Christ for the remission of sins, and ye shall receive the gift of the Holy Ghost. For the promise is unto you, and to your children, and to all that are afar off, even as many as the LORD our God shall call. And with many other words did he testify and exhort, saying, Save yourselves from this untoward generation. Then they that gladly received his word were baptized: and the same day there were added unto them about three thousand souls." (Acts 2:38-41)*

After Pentecost then came the salvation to the gentiles through Cornelius the centurion and his entire household:

> *"To him give all the prophets witness, that through his name whosoever believeth in him shall receive remission of sins. While Peter yet spake these words, the Holy Ghost fell on all them which heard the word. And they of the circumcision which believed were astonished, as many as came with Peter, because that on the Gentiles also was poured out the gift of the Holy Ghost." (Acts 10:43)*

After Cornelius was saved then the prison keeper and his household were saved. (Acts 10:43-45) I could go on and on concerning the records of souls being saved, but you get the idea. In addition to the book of Acts written by the physician Luke what about all of the epistles (letters) written by the Apostle Paul to church leaders across the region filled with converts that were a result of Paul's ministry. We are talking about thousands and thousands of lost souls that had been redeemed and yet there is no mention that any of these people ever lost their salvation or ever had a need to be saved again. Some of the Books in the New Testament remain with the author being unknown, but most theologians believe that Paul wrote fourteen of the twenty seven New Testament books. One would have to conclude therefore, that either it is simply not possible to lose your salvation or, if it were possible, that it never did happen to anyone as for as the scriptures are concerned. We do know that it would be impossible to be saved again if you could lose it, because Christ would have to be sacrificed again. (Heb 6:6) Nevertheless, I believe if that situation had ever occurred that surely somebody would have made note of it. Again, your salvation was not earned by you and it's not kept by you, God gave it to you and God keeps it for you.

Winning Souls for Christ

Since we are on the topic of the importance of your testimony and the mission of winning people over to Christ I would like to share some other thoughts that the Holy Spirit gave me on winning souls. For those of you who consider yourselves to be soul-winners. First let me say you are not soul-winners you are husbandmen or farmers and you do not win souls that is what God does. You plant seeds and you fertilize the seed and you water the seed and you pull out the weeds. Every now and then you are lucky enough for God to allow you to be there when the seed is ready to be harvested, but it is God that gives the increase not the mouth piece that He chose to partake of the fruit.

> *"For while one saith, I am of Paul; and another, I am of Apollos; are ye not carnal? Who then is Paul, and who is Apollos, but ministers by whom ye believed, even as the Lord gave to every man? I have planted, Apollos watered; but God gave the increase. So then neither is he that planteth any thing, neither he that watereth; but God that giveth the increase. Now he that planteth and he that watereth are one: and every man shall receive his own reward according to his own labour. For we are labourers together with God: ye are God's husbandry, ye are God's building." (1Cor 3:4-9)*

One other thing I would like to mention concerning reaching people for Christ. Don't be discouraged in your efforts to lead people to Christ, but understand that not everyone will come to God. God will have mercy on those whom He will have mercy.

> *"For he saith to Moses, I will have mercy on whom I will have mercy, and I will have compassion on whom I will have compassion. So then it is not of him that willeth, nor of him that runneth, but of God that sheweth mercy. For the scripture saith unto Pharaoh, Even for this same purpose have I raised thee up, that I might shew my power in thee, and that my name might be declared throughout all the earth. Therefore hath he mercy on whom he will have mercy, and whom he will he hardeneth. Thou wilt say then unto me, Why doth he yet find fault? For who hath resisted his will? Nay but, O man, who art thou that repliest against God? Shall the thing formed say to him that formed it, Why hast thou made me thus? Hath not the potter power over the clay, of the same lump to make one vessel unto honour, and another unto dishonour? (Rom 9:15-21)*

Hardened Hearts

Some will never listen to you because their hearts are hardened and they don't want to hear anything about God. Jesus even warned His Apostles that some would not receive them when they tried to bring them the gospel. (Matt 10:14) Jesus told them to just shake the dust off of their feet and move on. You cannot talk to anyone about God who God has not prepared to receive it. You are wasting your time trying. These people will just argue with you about insignificant issues and you will never change their minds. This type of situation is not beneficial for anyone. I remember being so frustrated about this at one time because I had such a compassion for lost souls. I remember thinking when a doctor or a lawyer goes to school to learn their trade people listen to them, but not if you are a preacher. Then it dawned on me that people don't go to see doctors or lawyers unless they are in a position where they actually need one. People are not going to go to someone to listen to the gospel until they reach a point in their lives where they realize that they need one. So if you are one who is trying to serve God in this way, don't be discouraged, this is all part of God's plan. Some will never listen, some will come around after God works on them for a while and every once in a while you will come across a lost soul that is ready to drop off the vine; they just need someone to guide them through it. If Christians will let their lights shine brightly in this dark world, when God has that person ready they will come to the light. I'm not trying to speak in parables like Jesus did here, but we have already talked about these things to some degree and there is no better way to describe it. If you want to catch fish, put a bright light over the water when it is dark outside and the fish will be drawn to the light. The brighter the light shines the more fish will come. After all, Jesus has made us fishers of men. You should strive to be a bright light shining in a dark world, but remember even fish do not come to the light unless they are hungry.

"And he saith unto them, Follow me, and I will make you fishers of men." (Matt 4:19)

"And Jesus said unto them, Come ye after me, and I will make you to become fishers of men." (Mk 1:17)

Chapter Twenty One

Predestination

God Already Knew We Would Be Saved

Our salvation was already planned and secured by God in His foreknowledge before were even born. The doctrine of predestination is one that can be confusing and misinterpreted to mean something that it doesn't. The Calvanist believe that the doctrine of predestination means that from the foundation of the world it was predetermined who would go to hell and who would go to heaven and therefore it doesn't matter what you do with Jesus or the gospel, or how you live your life. Regardless of what you do with Jesus or with your life it has already been decided long before you were born what would be your eternal destiny. I believe this is an extreme interpretation and even though there is some truth in this interpretation I do not believe this is what God means in His Word.

If this were true, then there would be no need for the sacrifice of Jesus, there would be no need for the Word of God. There would be no need for preaching or the Gospel. There would be no need for a plan to save the world.

Foreknowledge

I think what they are referring to is the foreknowledge of God concerning what the eventual fate of every person born will be. It is true that God knows everything about you even before you are born. It is also true that God is all powerful and He is in control of everything, so it only makes sense to believe that your destiny is in the hands of God regardless of what you do or how you live. Herein is the problem. God created man in His own image and for His glory. It is a known fact that God does not control what man does because man was created with a free will. As we have seen, even after you are saved and possess the Holy Spirit, you are still not controlled by God, but you must surrender to God's will. It pleases God when we choose right, but we are never forced to do so. Does it please a puppeteer when his creation (the puppet) moves the way he moves him? No, because the puppet simply has no choice. Does it please us when our husbands or wives do the things we want them to? Yes, because they are doing it for our pleasure because they want to please us, but they didn't have to. They did it by choice. If

God is completely in control of our destiny, then man really doesn't have a choice and that is contrary to everything the Bible teaches. The focus is on the word predestination rather on the foreknowledge of God. It is only predetermined by God were man will end up because God knows what decisions we will make concerning the plan of salvation before we make it. From God's view point it is predetermined what our destiny is only because He knows ahead of time what decision we will make. It is therefore still the person that made the decision not God.

Knowledge Doesn't Mean Control

Don't confuse knowledge with control. Just because God knows ahead of time what decision each person will make doesn't mean that He controls that decision. It does mean however, that from God's perspective, He does know who will accept Christ as their savior and who will reject Him before they actually do it. When we are talking about predestination, or the chosen, or the elect, or the called, or those who were written in the Lambs Book of Life before the foundation of the world we are talking about from God's perspective not from a man's. God knows this ahead of time, but we do not. God does not control man or his decision to accept or deny Christ ahead of time, but He does know what decision we will make. Now let's look at some of the verses pertaining to God's foreknowledge:

> *"Before I formed you in the womb I knew you, before you were born I set you apart; I appointed you as a prophet to the nations."*
> *(Jer 1:5)*

This verse illustrates that God knows each and every person, who they are and who they will become and what they will do with their lives even prior to their births.

> *"To those who are the elect exiles of the Dispersion in Pontus, Galatia, Cappadocia, Asia and Bithynia, who have been chosen according to the foreknowledge of God the Father, through the sanctifying work of the Spirit, to be obedient to Jesus Christ and sprinkled with his blood: Grace and peace be yours in abundance."* (1 Pet 1:1-2)

This verse clearly states that these people had been chosen according to the foreknowledge of God the Father to be sanctified by the Spirit and sprinkled with the blood of Christ. They were chosen in advance to become children of God the Father by accepting Christ. God did not make them get saved, but with His foreknowledge God the Father knew in advance that they would. Even though God the Father, as our creator, would have the right to make that choice for mankind, I don't believe this is what is being stated here. It is mankind that makes the choice, but God already knows what choice each man is going to make.

Knowing something is going to happen is not the same thing as causing it to happen. Now let's look at some verses that deal with the term "Predestination":

Predestination

> *"According as he hath chosen us in him before the foundation of the world, that we should be holy and without blame before him in love: Having predestinated us unto the adoption of children by Jesus Christ to himself, according to the good pleasure of his will." (Eph 1:4-5)*

Those who choose Christ for salvation are predestined by God to become children of God through adoption into God's family by the indwelling of the Holy Spirit. Since we know man has free will to choose or refuse salvation I believe God is saying that what happens to a person after they accept Christ has already been predetermined. They will be children of God and they will be conformed to the image of Christ.

> *"In whom we also have obtained an inheritance, being predestinated according to the purpose of him who worketh all things after the counsel of his own will: That we should be to the praise of his glory, who first trusted in Christ." (Eph 1:11-12)*

Of course God will ensure that all things turn out according to His plans regarding those who have accepted Christ and also for those who do not. We are predestined only by the fact that God already knows what we will do concerning these things. As far as God is concerned, these decisions have already been made because He knows what we will do. From the foundation of the world God already knew you and already knew what choices you would make.

The Called

Those whom God already knows that they are going to accept His gift of eternal life are called to the Son (Jesus) by the Father.

> *"For many are called, but few are chosen." (Matt 22:14)*
>
> *"These shall make war with the Lamb, and the Lamb shall overcome them: for he is Lord of lords and King of kings: and they that are with him are called, and chosen, and faithful." (Rev 17:14)*
>
> *"Who hath saved us, and called us with an holy calling, not according to our works, but according to his own purpose and grace, which was given us in Christ Jesus before the world began,"*
>
> *"All things are delivered to me of my Father: and no man knoweth who the Son is, but the Father, and who the Father is but the Son, and he to whom the Son will reveal him."*

All of these verses are telling us that God the Father knew who would be saved before they were even born. Those whom He knew would be saved He called them to come to the Son to receive their salvation. That doesn't mean that only the ones that were going to accept Christ were called, but it does mean that those who have accepted Christ were called. In God's eyes these are the chosen and the elect because God knew they would accept His Son as their savior even prior to the foundation of the world. The verses that wrap all this up in a nice clean package using all of these terms together is in the book of Romans:

> *"And we know that all things work together for the good to them that love God, to them who are the called according to his purpose. For whom he did foreknow, he also did predestinate to be conformed to the image of his Son, that he might be the firstborn among many brethren. Moreover whom he did predestinate, them he also called: and whom he called, them he also justified: and whom he justified, them he also glorified." (Rom 8:28-30)*

God Already Knows Who Will be Saved

Whether a person believes that predestination is God the Father deciding ahead of time who is going to heaven and who is going to hell, or simply the fact that the Father knows ahead of time who will be going to heaven or hell doesn't really matter for our conversation. What we do know for sure is that predestination is a Biblical doctrine and therefore it should be included in our conversation. Based on the verses that we have seen here we know that due to the foreknowledge of God He has known for eternity, even before the foundation of the world, who would be saved and who would not. From God the Father's perspective then, the people who have been or even, will be saved before the end of the church age, are already written in the Lambs book of life. For God the past, present, and future all just as much a reality as the past and the present are for us. I said earlier that when you are born the natural birth your name is written in the book of life and when you are born the spiritual birth your name is written in the Lambs book of life. From man's perspective, with his limitations concerning the future, this is absolutely true, but to God the future is just as much present tense as the present is to us.

All Part of God's Plan

All of these facts point to one simple conclusion for the sake of our conversation; To God the Father, the fact that we will be born a natural birth is a matter of history. He knows the date, the time, the instant that this event took place. He knows ahead of time, for every person, when it did happen, or when it will happen. This is not something that comes and goes. When it happens it is recorded in God's book. Your spiritual birth is the same way. It is an event that God knows ahead of time exactly when you were, or will be saved by the spiritual birth and when that time comes your name will be recorded in the Lambs book of life. For God, who has no concept of time this has already happened, but for us it might well be still a future event. I don't believe God chooses who will be saved and who will not because the entire Bible teaches it will be mankind's choice to accept or refuse the gospel of Jesus Christ. I do believe that God knows ahead of time who will accept Christ and who will not, but He does not influence or control these decisions. If He did He would make everyone believe. The verse above says that those who have been saved are predestined to become like Jesus and we know that this will happen. When the rapture takes place we will be transformed and we will receive glorified bodies and we will understand all things because we will be like Jesus with our glorified, celestial bodies and our indwelling of the Spirit of God within us. The verse says this is all done according to God's purpose. What is God's purpose? We may not understand all of it, but this verse gives us the main part. That through the redeeming work of Jesus on the cross and the indwelling of the Holy Spirit, it is God's plan and purpose to have His family all together with Him in heaven. Through this process Jesus has become the firstborn of many brethren that will or have already become the children of God and God will take them home and He will be their God and they will be His people. This has been God's plan all along. With this in mind, it is silly to even suggest that you can be saved, and become a child of God, and have your name written in the Lambs book of life, and be born spiritually into God's family, and believe that you could lose that special place of privilege that God, who knows all things past, present and future, has already given you and has recorded it in His records. Yes to God you are the chosen, you are the elect, you are the called, and not because God chose you, but because God knew that you would choose Him. We love God because He first loved us. (1Jn 4:19)

Chapter Twenty Two

Ambassadors for Christ

Ambassadors for Christ

This topic dealing with the subject of ambassadors is very similar to the chapter concerning the children of God being a light in a lost world. That topic however, was talking about how Christians should present themselves to the world in relation to winning souls while being an ambassador speaks more about being a representative for Christ. The word "Ambassador" comes from the Greek word "Presbeuo" (pres-byoo'-o) which means to act as a representative, it sometimes refers to a senior in the faith or a preacher. God does not call all Christians to be preachers, but He does expect all of us be His representatives on this earth. We should all strive to become seniors in the faith or mature Christians that are ready and able to give an answer to all those who would question us about the hope that is within us. Since we are ambassadors or, representatives of Christ, we should strive to do everything the same way that Christ would do it. I recently read a book called "In His Steps" by Charles Sheldon. In this book the pastor of a church challenged his people in his congregation to try to make every decision in their lives and in their businesses the way they thought Jesus would. It is quite a story how it all turned out. This is what I am talking about, if we are to represent Christ on earth then every decision we make should be made the way Jesus would make it. That being said, if we live for Jesus and try to represent Jesus, how would it look to the world if we were representing Jesus one day, and then all of a sudden we are lost again and now we are representing Satan. I know we don't always live the way we should, or act the way we should, but I also know that if you are a child of God you do act different than those who are not and the world around you can tell the difference. Our main job as representatives of Christ is to reconcile, that is, to restore the relationship between God and man that was destroyed at the fall of man.

> *"And all things are of God, who hath reconciled us to himself by Jesus Christ, and hath given to us the ministry of reconciliation; To wit, that God was in Christ, reconciling the world unto himself, not imputing their trespasses unto them; and hath committed unto us the*

> *word of reconciliation. Now then we are ambassadors for Christ, as though God did beseech you by us: we pray you in Christ's stead, be ye reconciled to God. For he hath made him to be sin for us, who knew no sin; that we might be made the righteousness of God in him." (2Cor 5:18-21)*

> *"And for me, that utterance may be given unto me, that I may open my mouth boldly, to make known the mystery of the gospel, For which I am an ambassador in bonds: that therein I may speak boldly, as I ought to speak." (Eph 6:19-20)*

You Are the Body of Christ

You as a Christian are a representative to the world for Jesus Christ. As I've mentioned before, you are the only part of God that man can see physically because you are the body of Christ and one with God. It is through your living testimony, through your ability to allow people to see the power of God in you, that God reaches the world and draws people to His Son Jesus for salvation. It is through the power of the Holy Spirit that lives inside of you that God spreads the gospel of Jesus Christ and convicts hearts to prepare them to receive His gift of eternal life. How are you doing? Can people see God in you? Do you do your part in showing God (the light of the world) to the people who live in the darkness of the world?

Again, I say that my salvation is secure in God because of what it would do to God's mission in this world, to seek out lost souls, if I, being God's own representative, could be a witness to all the miraculous things that God has done for me one day and be as lost as those I had been witnessing to the next day. How appealing is a gospel that only saves you occasionally when you feel like being godly? Even the lost people in the world know they do not want a salvation that only works when they feel like playing the part. If this were possible the gospel would have never spread and the church would never have gone anywhere. Can you imagine what it would have been like if even one of the people in the early church had lost their salvation and had gone back to their sinful lives. We all know there have been many people who have played the part for a while and then turned back, but we also know that those people, according to God's Word, were never saved to begin with. (1 Jn 2:19) Sometimes it is difficult to tell if you are dealing with a backslidden Christian (someone who was really saved but has temporarily lost their way) and someone who was never saved to begin with, but was only playing the part. The Bible says if they are only playing the part and they were never saved, then they will eventually leave and this is how we know. There would be no church, there would be no salvation, there would be no redemption through the blood of Christ, and there would be no Christian testimony. This alone is sufficient reason for God to hold on to our salvation for us and not trust man to keep it. I know that I have repeated myself several times; this is because, for one thing, repetition is the key to learning and hopefully you will not forget the things that you have learned concerning eternal security. Another reason is because this is how the Word of God explains what God has done for us. It would not be sufficient to just tell you that Jesus died on the cross to pay for your sins. When Jesus died He fulfilled so many prophesies that it would take forever to comment on all of them. This is God's way of proving that Jesus is the savior of the world and the only hope for mankind. All of these things are intertwined together and therefore when they are explained it appears to be saying the same thing over and over. The only thing that is important is that you understand that Jesus is who He says He is, that He can do for you what He said He could do and that you believe that with all your might and surrender your heart to Him. You should be able to see by now that the entire Bible teaches that our salvation cannot be lost. It is a central theme and message that all the passages of the Bible agree on. After all these things that I have shared with you already on this topic you should have reached the conclusion that if you read something in the Bible that doesn't seem to agree with this main theme then you must not be interpreting what the passage is conveying correctly. All scripture should be interpreted using other passages in God's Word to verify its meaning.

The Evidence

If you are truly a born again Christian, then your life should be different than it was before you were saved. This means that you should now have a desire to live a life that is pleasing to God. The Bible tells us that before God provided us with a means for salvation that each person did that which was right in his own eyes. (Judges 17:6) Generally this meant that each person only looked out for their own interest in this world. In today's society we are surrounded by those who worship the false gods of science, the false gods of materialism, the false gods of humanism, and the false gods of atheism. The fact is mankind can make anything their god. Bottom line is, if you place your faith in anything other than Jesus Christ, then you are placing your trust in a false god which means you are putting faith in the devil.

It should be evident to everyone if the Holy Spirit lives inside of you. It is not hard to see the contrast. In Galatians chapter five the works of the flesh are listed first and then the works of the Spirit after that. The contrast that can be seen between the two should be easy for anyone to see. Now let's look at these verses:

> *"This I say then, Walk in the Spirit, and ye shall not fulfil the lust of the flesh. For the flesh lusteth against the Spirit, and the Spirit against the flesh: and these are contrary the one to the other: so that ye cannot do the things that ye would. But if*

ye be led of the Spirit, ye are not under the law." (Gal 5:16-18)

"Now the works of the flesh are manifest, which are these; Adultery, fornication, uncleanness, lasciviousness, Idolatry, witchcraft, hatred, variance, emulations, wrath, strife, seditions, heresies, Envyings, murders, drunkenness, revellings, and such like: of the which I tell you before, as I have also told you in time past, that they which do such things shall not inherit the kingdom of God." (Gal 5:19-21)

"But the fruit of the Spirit is love, joy, peace, longsuffering, gentleness, goodness, faith, Meekness, temperance: against such there is no law. And they that are Christ's have crucified the flesh with the affections and lusts. If we live in the Spirit, let us also walk in the Spirit." (Gal 5:22-25)

The Christian Legitimacy Test

If the things listed above as works of the flesh describe your behavior in this world, then you should seriously considered the legitimacy of your salvation, that is, if you claim to be a Christian. I know some folks whom this description fits quite well, fortunately they are not people who ever claimed to be saved and they are not people I socialize with. On the hand, if the things listed here as fruits of the Spirit are a more accurate description of you or others that you know, then it is pretty safe to say that they are good representatives or ambassadors of Christ. This passage of scripture Gal 5:16-24 is what I like to call "The Christianity Legitimacy Test". Now I'm not saying that if you are saved that you will never do anything that is in the list under works of the flesh, I'm talking about a change of heart. I think a lot of things will change quickly, but it may take a while to root out all of the fleshly habits that you have developed before you were saved. The thing is, you should have a desire in your heart to change these things if you are saved. If you fail to be able to resist some of the temptations that are presented to you, you will immediately feel guilty because you will grieve the Holy Spirit that now lives inside of you. If this does not happen when you sin against God, then maybe the Holy Spirit isn't there and if not, then you are not saved. Jesus proclaimed repeatedly that ye shall know them by their fruits.

> *"Ye shall know them by their fruits. Do men gather grapes of thorns, or figs of thistles? Even so every good tree bringeth forth good fruit; but a corrupt tree bringeth forth evil fruit. A good tree cannot bring forth evil fruit, neither can a corrupt tree bring forth good fruit. Every tree that bringeth not forth good fruit is hewn down, and cast into the fire. Wherefore by their fruits ye shall know them. Not every one that saith unto me, Lord, Lord, shall enter into the kingdom of heaven; but he that doeth*

> *the will of my Father which is in heaven. Many will say to me in that day, Lord, Lord, have we not prophesied in thy name? and in thy name have cast out devils? and in thy name done many wonderful works, And then will I profess unto them, I never knew you: depart from me, ye that work iniquity." (Matt 7:16-23)*
>
> *Additional references: Jn 15:1-8*

Religious But Lost

In these verses Jesus is talking to the religious leaders who claimed to know God, but they did not live a life for God. They did good deeds in front of men, to be seen of men, not because they loved God. Jesus told them not everyone who claims to be godly is actually saved. Even if they claim to know God and don't walk the walk of a godly person, then they are not of God, and they will not enter the kingdom of God. It is the same way with Christians. Unfortunately, there will be many out there who do things in the name of religion or in the name of God, but they really don't know God and they will not go to heaven. As an ambassador for Christ, not only do we represent Christ, but we also represent God the Father, the Holy Spirit, Heaven (since through Christ is the only way to get there), everlasting life and the only escape from hell and the lake of fire that God has provided for mankind. You, as the representative of Christ, are mankind's only avenue to salvation.

Chapter Twenty Three

Led by the Spirit

Walking in the Spirit

When the Holy Spirit lives inside you, He will guide you into righteousness, but He will not control you. The Holy Spirit will only lead as much of your life as you are willing to surrender to Him. In the following verses Jesus describes to us how a person who is led by the Spirit lives. This is referred to as walking in the Spirit.

> *"Ye have heard that it hath been said, An eye for an eye, and a tooth for a tooth: Matthew, But I say unto you, That ye resist not evil: but whosoever shall smite thee on thy right cheek, turn to him the other also. And if any man will sue thee at the law, and take away thy coat, let him have thy cloak also. And whosoever shall compel thee to go a mile, go with him twain. Give to him*

that asketh thee, and from him that would borrow of thee turn not thou away. Ye have heard that it hath been said, Thou shalt love thy neighbour, and hate thine enemy. But I say unto you, Love your enemies, bless them that curse you, do good to them that hate you, and pray for them which despitefully use you, and persecute you; That ye may be the children of your Father which is in heaven: for he maketh his sun to rise on the evil and on the good, and sendeth rain on the just and on the unjust. For if ye love them which love you, what reward have ye? do not even the publicans the same? And if ye salute your brethren only, what do ye more than others? do not even the publicans so? Be ye therefore perfect, even as your Father which is in heaven is perfect." (Matt 5:38-48)

In the world that we live in today this kind of thinking is unheard of. I seldom here this kind of preaching in the churches today, but this is how God wants us to live. Keeping God's laws should not be difficult or seem strange to a Christian. We should do it because we love God and want to live a life that is pleasing to Him. Every day I hear people talking about suing someone, or getting even with someone. I often find myself biting my tongue knowing that this is how the world is today. I feel like a stranger in a foreign land most of the time. I get tired of people saying things like, "Why are you being nice to me, what do you want?" or "Okay so what are you not telling me or hiding from me." Why does everyone have hidden motives and lives that are filled with deceit? If you are a Christian these things should not be true of you, you should be different than the world. I have been sued for nothing and I refused to fight back. In the end, someone else in the suit ended up paying a million dollars for something they were not responsible for. Everyone is looking for a get rich quick scheme or trying to win the lottery, or gambling in an effort to escape real work. Just like blessings and cursing from the same mouth, these things ought not be so, but they are. (Jms 3:10)

> *"Whosoever believeth that Jesus is the Christ is born of God: and every one that loveth him that begat loveth him also that is begotten of him. By this we know that we love the children of God, when we love God, and keep his commandments. For this is the love of God, that we keep his commandments: and his commandments are not grievous. For whatsoever is born of God overcometh the world: and this is the victory that overcometh the world, even our faith. Who is he that overcometh the world, but he that believeth that Jesus is the Son of God?" (Jn 5:1-5)*

Two Kinds of Baptism

When Christians commit sins it grieves the Holy Spirit that lives inside of them and immediately produces guilt and remorse. Doing good works, keeping God's laws, or obeying God's commandments, all mean the same thing. Doing this is evidence that they are the children of God. The first step of obedience for a child of God is baptism. I am speaking of being baptized by water as Jesus commanded us to do, but before I explain what baptism by water is, I should clarify that the Word of God talks about two different types of baptism, and this sometimes confuses people. The first baptism that a Christian experiences is the baptism of the Holy Ghost and the second should be the baptism in water. Before Jesus began His ministry, His cousin John the Baptist, was sent by God to prepare the way of the Lord as it had been prophesied in the Old Testament. John proclaimed that he had been sent to prepare people for the coming of Jesus Christ. To those who displayed a repentant heart for their sinful lives he, John the Baptist, baptized them in water. As you know repentance is required before a person is prepared to receive Christ as their savior. This water baptism of John signified the same thing then as it does now. It is a picture of a person's repentance for being a sinner and the acceptance of their willingness to die to their sinful lifestyles in order to rise again to live a life for God. John told his disciples that he was sent to prepare the way of the Lord and that he baptized with the baptism of repentance and with water, but one would come whom he was not worthy to even unbuckle His shoes, who would baptize with the Holy Ghost.

> *"The beginning of the gospel of Jesus Christ, the Son of God; As it is written in the prophets, Behold, I send my messenger before thy face, which shall prepare thy way before thee. The voice of one crying in the wilderness, Prepare ye the way of the Lord, make his paths straight. John did baptize in the wilderness, and preach the baptism of repentance for the remission of sins. And there went out unto him all the land of Judaea, and they of Jerusalem, and were all baptized of him in the river of Jordan, confessing their sins. And John was clothed with camel's hair, and with a girdle of a skin about his loins; and he did eat locusts and wild honey; And preached, saying, There cometh one mightier than I after me, the latchet of whose shoes I am not worthy to stoop down and unloose. I indeed have baptized you with water: but he shall baptize you with the Holy Ghost. (Mk 1:1-8)*
>
> *Additional References: Mt 3:11, Lk 3:16, Acts 1:5, Acts 11:16*

The word "Baptize" here is the Greek word "*Baptizo*" (bap-tid'-so) which means to be whelmed, fully covered with a liquid, to be fully wet. That is why when a person is Baptized in water they should be fully immersed. This is also true because baptism in water is an outward expression of an inward action. It is a picture to the world of your death to the worldly life of the flesh to rise again to a life dedicated to God. When you are baptized in water you are buried in the likeness of Jesus' death and raised again in the likeness of His resurrection to walk in newness of life.

> *"Know ye not, that so many of us as were baptized into Jesus Christ were baptized into his death? Therefore we are buried with him by baptism into death: that like as Christ was raised up from the dead by the glory of the Father, even so we also should walk in newness of life. For if we have been planted together in the likeness of his death, we shall be also in the likeness of his resurrection: Knowing this, that our old man is crucified with him, that the body of sin might be destroyed, that henceforth we should not serve sin. For he that is dead is freed from sin. Now if we be dead with Christ, we believe that we shall also live with him: Knowing that Christ being raised from the dead dieth no more; death hath no more dominion over him. For in that he died, he died unto sin once: but in that he liveth, he liveth unto God. Likewise reckon ye also yourselves to be dead indeed unto sin, but alive unto God through Jesus Christ our Lord." (Rom 6:3-11)*

Baptized With the Holy Spirit

Jesus never baptized anyone with water other than his disciples. (Jn 4:2) It is obvious then, that the baptism with water is not the same as the baptism of the Holy Ghost. It is important to understand this because there are some out there who believe that you must be baptized in water in order to be saved. Baptism with water is not part of salvation, but the baptism with the Holy Spirit is. When you believe the gospel of Jesus Christ, that is the plan of salvation, and confess your faith in Him you immediately receive the Holy Ghost, you become indwelt by the Holy Spirit of God. This is called the baptism of the Holy Ghost. If you have not been baptized by the Holy Ghost then you are not saved. If you are saved and have not been baptized in water then you should be. If you were baptized in water before you were baptized with the Holy Ghost, then all you did was get wet. Baptism in water does not and cannot save you. I don't believe in baptizing infants because they have not reached an age where they can acknowledge their need for a savior (age of accountability). They have not repented for being a sinner. They cannot understand the plan of salvation and they cannot accept Christ as their savior.

The Bible does not mention anyone being baptized with the Holy Ghost until after Jesus was glorified (He received His purified or Celestial body, and ascended into heaven). Jesus told His disciples that the Holy

Spirit was with them before he ascended, but the Holy Spirit would be in them after He went to heaven and sent the Holy Spirit to them. I don't expect you to take my word for anything so I have included the verses here:

> *"And, behold, I send the promise of my Father upon you: but tarry ye in the city of Jerusalem, until ye be endued with power from on high." (Lk 24:49)*
>
> *"But when the Comforter is come, whom I will send unto you from the Father, even the Spirit of truth, which proceedeth from the Father, he shall testify of me:" (Jn 15:26)*
>
> *"Nevertheless I tell you the truth; It is expedient for you that I go away: for if I go not away, the Comforter will not come unto you; but if I depart, I will send him unto you." (Jn 16:7)*
>
> *"And, being assembled together with them, commanded them that they should not depart from Jerusalem, but wait for the promise of the Father, which, saith he, ye have heard of me. For John truly baptized with water; but ye shall be baptized with the Holy Ghost not many days hence. When they therefore were come together, they asked of him, saying, Lord, wilt thou at this time restore again the kingdom to Israel? And he said unto them, It is not for you to know the times or the seasons, which the Father hath*

> *put in his own power. But ye shall receive power, after that the Holy Ghost is come upon you: and ye shall be witnesses unto me both in Jerusalem, and in all Judaea, and in Samaria, and unto the uttermost part of the earth." (Acts 1:4-8)*

Baptism with the Holy Ghost happens when you are saved; baptism with water should be your first step of obedience as a new born Christian. Baptism with the Holy Spirit should come first. Following are a number of passages that illustrate the fact the baptism with water only happens after baptism with the Holy Spirit.

> *"To him give all the prophets witness, that through his name whosoever believeth in him shall receive remission of sins. While Peter yet spake these words, the Holy Ghost fell on all them which heard the word. And they of the circumcision which believed were astonished, as many as came with Peter, because that on the Gentiles also was poured out the gift of the Holy Ghost. For they heard them speak with tongues, and magnify God. Then answered Peter, Can any man forbid water, that these should not be baptized, which have received the Holy Ghost as well as we? And he commanded them to be baptized in the name of the Lord. Then prayed they him to tarry certain days." (Acts 10:43-48)*

> *"Then Philip opened his mouth, and began at the same scripture, and preached unto him Jesus. And as they went on their way, they came unto a certain water: and the eunuch said, See, here is water; what doth hinder me to be baptized? And Philip said, If thou believest with all thine heart, thou mayest. And he answered and said, I believe that Jesus Christ is the Son of God. And he commanded the chariot to stand still: and they went down both into the water, both Philip and the eunuch; and he baptized him. And when they were come up out of the water, the Spirit of the Lord caught away Philip, that the eunuch saw him no more: and he went on his way rejoicing." (Acts 8:35-39)*

Some theologians teach that there is a third type of baptism. They are referring to the baptism with fire as seen in Matt 3:11. The fire that is spoken of in this verse is referring to the refining or purification that takes place when the Holy Spirit indwells the believer and therefore this is all talking about the same event. Spirit and fire are inseparable because the body must be purged or purified of any demonic influence prior to the indwelling of the Spirit of God.

Trying to Live For God

In both of the examples given in these scriptures it is obvious that the new believers could not be baptized with water until they had believed in the gospel and had received the Holy Spirit. If baptism with water were required for salvation, then this would not be possible. We get baptized with the Holy Ghost and with fire when we are saved and then we get baptized in water because we are saved. If you are led by the Spirit, then you know what I'm talking about. You have accepted Christ and even though you may not recall the exact date, you remember doing it and you know how it changed your life. Since that time you have strived to live for God though you may not have always done the right thing in the long run, it is your desire to live a life that is pleasing to God. You have a desire to know what God's will is and to do what God wants you to do. These things are evidence that you are a child of God, if you feel this way, I believe there is a good chance that you have been saved and are still saved. You may not always feel close to God. You need to understand that our relationship to God is not based on feelings, it is based on faith. The whole purpose of this book is to reassure you that if you have accepted Christ as your savior, no matter what has happened since then, you are still a child of God. If you have strayed away from fellowship with God, then I will bet that each day you can feel the Holy Spirit tugging on your heart for you to come back to God. This does not mean that you have lost your salvation. It means that you have drifted away from experiencing the fellowship with God that you should be having on a daily basis, and you only need to ask God to forgive you and come back to Him.

> *"If we confess our sins, he is faithful and just to forgive us of our sins, and to cleanse us from all unrighteousness." (1 Jn 1:9)*

CHAPTER TWENTY FOUR

Born Again

Definition

Out of all of the things that we have discussed, out of all the reasons that I have given you why I believe our salvation is secure for all of eternity, perhaps this one is the most profound. Look what Jesus says to the religious leader Nicodemus in the book of John Chapter three:

> *"Jesus answered and said unto him, Verily, verily, I say unto thee, Except a man be born again, he cannot see the kingdom of God."*
> *(Jn 3:3)*

In order to help you see and comprehend the significance of these words I am going to give you the definitions from the Strong's concordance of the Bible. First the word "Born", it is the Greek word

"Gennao" (ghen-nah-o). This word is defined as "to procreate, to regenerate, to bear or beget, to bring forth or to conceive". I don't believe the word "Born" comes with any amazement, but now let us look at the word "Again". The word "Again" is the Greek word "Anothen" (an-o-then), this word is defined as either to repeat, which is the way in which it is normally translated, or it can be translated to mean: "to come from above, to be from the highest, to descend from the top". So if you take the meanings of these two words and combine them as Jesus did, I think we get a clearer picture of what Jesus was actually trying to make Nicodemus understand. In order for anyone to be able to see the kingdom of God they must be, procreated from above, begat from the highest place, conceived from the top. Jesus is talking about becoming a child of God through the indwelling of the Holy Spirit that occurs when you accept Christ as your savior. This is how God creates His children. We are the offspring of God through the conception of the Holy Spirit. This is the same way that Jesus was conceived (by the Holy Ghost), only when Jesus was conceived by the Spirit He was still in His mother's womb.

> *"But while he thought on these things, behold, the angel of the Lord appeared unto him in a dream, saying, Joseph, thou son of David, fear not take unto the Mary thy wife: for that which is conceived in her is of the Holy Ghost." (Matt 1:20)*

So when we are saved, when we accept Christ as the Son of God and ask Him to be our savior, that is when we are conceived by the Holy Ghost and become the children of God.

Why Jesus Used the Word "Born".

I believe Jesus described this indwelling of the Holy Spirit as being born of the Spirit for several reasons which can be found in the following verses back in the Book of John:

> *"Nicodemus sayeth unto him, How can a man be born when he is old? Can he enter the second time into his mother's womb, and be born?" (Jn 3:4)*

The simple answer to Nicodemus' question is no of course not, but what does this answer implicate? What are the characteristics of being born?

1. You can only be conceived and born of a natural birth one time. You cannot go back into your mother's womb. You cannot become unborn; the unborn refers only to those who have not yet been born. You cannot put the toothpaste back into the tube. If you can only be born a natural birth one time, then the second birth must be referring to something supernatural or spiritual.

2. You cannot be only partially born. You have either been born or you have not been born. There is no in-between. You cannot be born just a little. You cannot be only a little pregnant. You are either pregnant or you're not pregnant, you are either born or not born. You have either received a natural birth, or you have not, you have either received a Spiritual birth, or you have not.
3. There is no method of undoing what has been done. You cannot wish to be unborn and all of a sudden you don't exist anymore. You cannot pray or beg to become unborn. No-one can take your life back after it has been given to you, not even your parents who are the ones who gave it to you to begin with. They can't take it back and you can't give it back. This is the nature of birth; it cannot be taken away once it has been given.

Natural birth verses Spiritual birth

In order to affirm that Jesus is referring to a natural or fleshly birth, and then a supernatural or Spiritual birth, He gives us the following two verses which make it perfectly clear:

> *"Jesus answered, Verily, verily, I say unto thee, Except a man be born of water and of the Spirit, he cannot enter into the Kingdom of God." (Jn 3:5)*

"That which is born of the flesh is flesh; and that which is born of the Spirit is spirit." (Jn 3:6)

I separated these two verses because there are a number of things I want to point out here. The word "Verily" is used by Jesus to point out only those things which are significantly important. The word can be translated truly, truly or sometimes "Amen" and is utilized to indicate emphasis or affirmation. Jesus is saying okay Nicodemus, pay attention to what I am about to tell you because this is very important. "Except a man be born of water", the water birth is clearly a reference to the natural birth, the water being the amniotic fluid that the unborn child lives in while still in the mother's womb. I'm sure you have heard of women say their water broke just prior to giving birth. Then it says, "And of the Spirit". I want you to notice that the "flesh" in the verse is not capitalized which means it is talking about a mortal being, while the word "Spirit" is capitalized which indicates deity. The first birth is from man and the second is from God. Not only does this verse show the deity of the Holy Spirit, but it also declares that He who has impregnated us with the Spirit of God is God the Father. For those who did not grasp this declaration by Christ in verse five Jesus reiterates the importance of this statement by rewording it, and stating it over again in verse six. The first birth is that of the flesh through your parents, the second birth is that of the Spirit (once again capitalized) is of God. In verses seven and eight Jesus tries to explain to Nicodemus how the Spirit of God operates since it was obvious to Him that Nicodemus was shocked and confused by what he had just heard.

How the Spirit Operates

> *"Marvel not that I said unto thee, Ye must be born again. The wind bloweth where it listeth, and thou hearest the sound there of, but cannot tell whence it cometh, and whither it goeth: so is everyone that is born of the Spirit." (Jn 3:7-8)*

Some things we don't need to fully understand how they operate to believe that they do exist. It is interesting that the word "Wind" used in verse eight is the Greek word "Pneuma" (pnyoo-mah), which can mean breath of life, current of airflow, a breeze, the Spirit of God, the Spirit of Christ or the Holy Spirit. Jesus is describing the operation of the Holy Spirit, but using the wind for an illustration that Nicodemus can understand. In the book of John chapter twenty and verse twenty two, the Bible says that Jesus breathed on the Apostles and said to them receive ye the Holy Ghost. When you receive the Holy Ghost you receive Spiritual life.

So, to summarize what this means we will once again look at the characteristics of birth but this time with the spiritual birth in mind:

1. Birth means to conceive or to begin something that wasn't there before, and in this case, it is referring to the beginning of spiritual life in the believer placed there by the Holy Spirit. Christians are the offspring of God because of the impregnation of the Spirit of God through the power and process of the Holy Spirit. The Holy Spirit cannot be given back to God by the receiver or taken back by God the giver. You cannot put the toothpaste back in to the tube.

2. Birth is an all or none concept. You cannot be only a little born of the Spirit. You are either fully born of God by the Spirit or you are not born of God. You cannot only have a little spiritual life. You are either spiritually alive or you are not. You cannot receive life and lose it and get it back. Once the spirit of man is removed from the body, the body is dead and is no longer supported by the breath of life. You cannot receive Spiritual life and lose it and get it back. Since the word death means to separate, then when the spirit of man separates from the body, the body is considered to be dead, but the spirit lives on either in hell or in heaven. This separation of the spirit from the body is the first death. If the spirit of man is then separated from the Spirit of God, then this second separation is the second death. If the spirit of man is conceived by the Holy Spirit, then that person

has received a second birth and therefore a second life. If this has happened, then that person cannot be separated from God because his spirit is now one with God's Spirit and they cannot ever be separated. He who is born twice, (of the flesh and of the Spirit) must only die once (be subject to only one death, the separation of the spirit from the body). He that is born only once (only has fleshly or natural life through their parents, but never received the second birth, or life through the Spirit of God) must die twice (the separation of the spirit from the body and the separation of their spirit from God for eternity). We are conceived of the Holy Ghost just like Jesus was, but we cannot be sinless like Jesus was because we were first conceived by our parents and therefore we carry the inheritance of sinful flesh from Adam. Jesus, on the other hand, was not conceived by sinful man, but rather His body and Spirit both came from God. We will receive sinless (Glorified or Celestial) bodies when we go to be with God in heaven. (1 Cor 15:40)

3. Being born a natural, or water birth, is not something that can be reversed by returning it to your parents. Your parents cannot take it back from you once it has been given. You cannot become unborn after that you have been born. Being born of the Spirit, or the

second birth, or a Spiritual birth, cannot be reversed by returning it to God. God cannot take it back from you once it has been given. You cannot become unborn again. I have heard people make fun of those who say salvation can't be lost by saying, "Some people believe that after you are saved you are going to heaven no matter what, even if God has to drag you there screaming and scratching all the way." If you think about it that is a silly thing to say. If you are saved then you know that at the end everyone's spirits will either go to hell or heaven. We also know, based on the Bible, what those two places will be like. It makes no sense to say that someone would scream and scratch and fight with God so they could go to hell instead of heaven. I don't believe it is possible to lose your salvation because of all the reasons I have given you in this book. I also don't believe that anyone will regret their decision to be saved when their time to depart arrives. We are safe and secure in the hands of God because it is not possible to be unborn again.

Chapter Twenty Five

The Devil Will Cause Doubt

Seeking Whom He May Devour

The devil will try every trick in the book to make you doubt whether or not you have ever been saved, and even more so, whether or not you have lost your salvation. It is his purpose on this earth to prevent as many people from being saved as possible. This world belongs to him and he wants to keep you with him. The devil's end is in the lake of fire and I know you don't want to end up there. Even if you have been saved, the devil cannot have your soul, but he can cause you to have doubts about your salvation and this will stifle your effectiveness in leading others to God. After I was first saved my preacher use to tell me that it took me twenty five years to become the sinner that I am, he said, you should not expect to change all of that in just a year or two. Boy was he ever right,

Safe and Secure in the Hands of Jesus

no matter how hard I tried, or how close I tried to be to God I found myself continuing to sin on some level every day. The fact is, as I've previously mentioned, there are two types of sinners, there are saved sinners and there are lost sinners. I have showed you how to become a child of God. I have showed you how that after you are saved you are indwelt with the power of the Holy Spirit. I have showed you how that you cannot lose your salvation because you are saved by God and your salvation is kept by God. I have showed you what God wants you to do with your life. So now you are thinking, I am a child of God now and all of my struggles are over with, oh how I wish that were true. There are a few flaws in that philosophy and I think you should be forewarned. First, the devil is still out there seeking whom he may devour and as a Christian you just became his primary target. That is because when you were lost you fit right in to the devil's dark world and you were of little concern to him.

> *"Ye do the deeds of your father. Then said they to him, We be not born of fornication; we have one Father, even God. Jesus said unto them, If God were your Father, ye would love me: for I proceeded forth and came from God; neither came I of myself, but he sent me. Why do ye not understand my speech? even because ye cannot hear my word. Ye are of your father the devil, and the lusts of your father ye will do. He was a murderer from the beginning, and abode not in the truth, because there is no truth*

> *in him. When he speaketh a lie, he speaketh of his own: for he is a liar, and the father of it." (Jn 8:41-44)*

> *"Be sober, be vigilant; because your adversary the devil, as a roaring lion, walketh about, seeking whom he may devour: (1Pet 5:8)*

Be Prepared to Fight the Devil

Now you have irritated him, first of all, because his desire for you was eternal damnation in hell along with him and his angels. As spoken by the demon Mephastophilis in the play "The Tragical History of Doctor Faustus" by Christopher Marlow in the 16th century, "Misery loves company". Now because you have accepted Christ he has lost the battle over your eternal soul and he isn't happy. He also knows that as a Christian God has one more servant, or tool to use against him for the battle of other souls that remain lost. The devil will throw everything he has in his arsenal at you now. Our fight in this world is against principalities and powers and darkness. You are now part of this spiritual battle. In order to be equipped to fight in this war you must put on the whole armor of God.

> *"Put on the whole armour of God, that ye may be able to stand against the wiles of the devil. For we wrestle not against flesh and blood, but against principalities, against*

powers, against the rulers of the darkness of this world, against spiritual wickedness in high places, Wherefore take unto you the whole armour of God, that ye may be able to withstand in the evil day, and having done all, to stand. Stand therefore, having your loins girt about with truth, and having on the breastplate of righteousness; And your feet shod with the preparation of the gospel of peace. Above all, taking the shield of faith, wherewith ye shall be able to quench all the fiery darts of the wicked. And take the helmet of salvation, and the sword of the Spirit, which is the word of God: Praying always with all prayer and supplication in the Spirit, and watching thereunto with all perseverance and supplication for all saints;" (Eph 6:11-18)

As you can see in the verses above, your weapons in this war are truth, righteousness, and the gospel, faith, salvation, the Word of God and prayer. You must put on the armor and you must learn how to use the armor against the devil.

The second reason is because the devil owns everything here. For now this world belongs to him and is under his control.

> *"Again, the devil taketh him up into an exceeding high mountain, and sheweth him all the kingdoms of the world, and the glory of them; And saith unto him, All these things will I give thee, if thou wilt fall down and worship me. Matt 4:8-9*

The devil will use all of his power, authority and possessions in order to try to get you to disobey God. There are few things I'd like to point out to you in the first ten verses of Mathew chapter four. This is when Jesus is tempted by the devil. First the Bible says that Jesus was led out by the Spirit of God to be tempted of the devil.

> *"Then was Jesus led up of the spirit into the wilderness to be tempted of the devil."* (Matt 4:1).

We Have a Proud Father

Doesn't that sound contradictory to everything that we have learned concerning the Holy Spirit? Was He not sent here to guide us into righteousness and help us overcome the devils temptations? Isn't it His job to keep our salvation secure until the day of redemption? So why would God (the Holy Spirit) lead anyone into a position where they would be tempted by the devil? Let me explain it this way. When my brother John and I were teenagers we were kind of scrawny looking but, we were both as strong as bulls. Two hundred pushups, one hundred sit ups and one hundred chin ups each night were pretty normal. He and I competed in exercise routines daily, and even though he usually won the competition, we were both in excellent shape. Whenever someone would threaten to fight one of us, or threaten anyone in our family, our father would have this saying prepared for them. "If you think you are man enough to handle one of them go ahead and jump on, but I'm not going to light a fire and try to smoke them off of you after you start it." Our father knew what would happen if someone accepted the challenge just like God the Father knew what would happen if the devil tried to tempt His Son Jesus. Remember God also allowed Job to be tested by the devil because God knew that Job would never turn his back on God no matter what the devil took from him. We have a proud God and He is proud of His children. Sometimes He will allow us to be tempted because He knows that He has prepared us to take on the devil and defeat him. He wants to show the world that the devil can be defeated by His children.

Next in these verses we can see the three areas where humans can be tempted by the devil. In verse three it is a human's basic need for survival. In this case it was food:

> *"And when the tempter came to him, he said, If thou be the Son of God, command that these stones be made bread." (Matt 4:3)*

In verses five and six we see the protection from physical harm:

> *"Then the devil taketh him up into the holy city, and setteth him on a pinnacle of the temple, And saith unto him, If thou be the Son of God, cast thyself down: for it is written, He shall give his angels charge*

> *concerning thee: and in their hands they shall bear thee up, lest at any time thou dash thy foot against a stone." (Matt 4:5-6)*

In verses eight and nine the temptation of worldly possessions:

> *"Again, the devil taketh him up into an exceeding high mountain, and sheweth him all the kingdoms of the world, and the glory of them; And saith unto him, All these things will I give thee, if thou wilt fall down and worship me." (Matt 4:8-9)*

In all three cases Jesus uses His armor and wards off the devil with the Word of God as can be seen in the following verses, four, seven and ten:

> *"But he answered and said, It is written, Man shall not live by bread alone, but by every word that proceedeth out of the mouth of God." (Matt 4:4)*

> *"Jesus said unto him, It is written again, Thou shalt not tempt the Lord thy God." (Matt 4:7)*

> *"Then saith Jesus unto him, Get thee hence, Satan: for it is written, Thou shalt worship the Lord thy God, and him only shalt thou serve." (Matt 4:10)*

Another Reason We Struggle With Sin

Another reason that we will struggle every day as Christians is because we still reside here on earth in our corrupt bodies. Right now my wife and I have two of our grand children living with us. They are such a blessing, yet I can understand why God intended for young children to be raised by young parents. I can't even begin to imagine what it must have been like for Abraham and Sarah to have a new born at the young ages of 100 and 90. Most of the time, we as grandparents just get to love on them and spoil them rotten for a short time while they are being little angels, and then send them home to their parents. However, if you keep them for very long your patience will soon run out. I don't have to tell you that they are born with rebellion in their bones. Don't get me wrong, I love them with all my heart, but sometimes they can test me to the limit. I know you have all heard of the terrible twos. Anyhow, we are all born with corruptible bodies. Ever wonder why you have to teach a child to be good, but you don't have to teach them how to be sinners. We are stuck in these corruptible, sinful, fleshly, immoral bodies even after we are saved and will continue to be until we die or the rapture comes. At that time we will be changed and will put on incorruption and we shall be like Jesus. I Cor 15:35-58. Flesh and blood cannot enter into the kingdom of God. The Apostle

Paul wrote about his continual struggle with the flesh in the Book of Romans chapter seven:

> *"For we know that the law is spiritual: but I am carnal, sold under sin. For that which I do I allow not: for what I would, that do I not; but what I hate, that do I. If then I do that which I would not, I consent unto the law that it is good. Now then it is no more I that do it, but sin that dwelleth in me. For I know that in me (that is, in my flesh,) dwelleth no good thing: for to will is present with me; but how to perform that which is good I find not. For the good that I would I do not: but the evil which I would not, that I do. Now if I do that I would not, it is no more I that do it, but sin that dwelleth in me. I find then a law, that, when I would do good, evil is present with me. For I delight in the law of God after the inward man: But I see another law in my members, warring against the law of my mind, and bringing me into captivity to the law of sin which is in my members. O wretched man that I am! who shall deliver me from the body of this death? I thank God through Jesus Christ our Lord. So then with the mind I myself serve the law of God; but with the flesh the law of sin." (Rom 7:14-25)*

Resist Temptation

In our minds and in our spirits we try to serve God but this is a daily struggle because sin still corrupts our worldly bodies. Never-the-less take comfort in these words; even though we may be led by the Holy Spirit to be tempted by the devil, even though we may be tempted every day by the devil by all that this world has to offer, even though we struggle every day with the sin that still dwells inside our corruptible bodies, God has promised us that He will not let us be tempted above that which we able to resist and with every temptation God will provide a path of escape.

> *"Wherefore let him that thinketh he standeth take heed lest he fall. There hath no temptation taken you but such as is common to man: but God is faithful, who will not suffer you to be tempted above that ye are able; but will with the temptation also make a way to escape, that ye may be able to bear it." (1Cor 10:12-13)*

Chapter Twenty Six

What if I Fall?

What is There to Keep Me from Sinning

So what will happen to me if I do give in to temptation even if God did provide me a way out and I didn't take it? Glad you asked, if we cannot lose our salvation even if we commit sins after that we are saved, then what is to keep us from living lives as though nothing has changed? First of all, if you are saved you will have a desire deep down in your soul to live a life that is pleasing to God. Second, God has given you the tools that you will need to resist temptations. If you continue a life of sin that is no different than it was before you were saved, then perhaps you were never saved to begin with because if you were, then the guilt inside of you caused by the grieving of the Holy Spirit would be more than you could live with. Many people who have professed to be Christians at one point in their lives have turned their backs on God. These people have a destiny which depends on what is in their hearts. If they truly were saved to begin with, then they will go one of two ways. First, they will eventually come back to God, or second, they will be taken out by God. I will explain that in a moment. If they were never saved to begin with, they will either get saved and get right with God, or they will end up in the lake of fire. There are many deceivers out in the world. Some have even deceived themselves. These people who are not saved, but are merely pretenders, will eventually leave the Christian family, when they do, that is how we will know they were never saved to begin with. Look at these verses:

> *"Little children, it is the last time: and as ye have heard that antichrist shall come, even now are there many antichrists; whereby we know that it is the last time. They went out from us, but they were not of us; for if they had been of us, they would no doubt have continued with us: but they went out, that they might be made manifest that they were not all of us." (Jn 2:18-19)*

God Disciplines His Children

If you truly are saved, and yet you continue to live in sin without remorse, then God will punish you the same way your parents punished you for disobedience as a child. The Bible says "Spare the rod, spoil the child." (Pr 13:24) It was God who gave that advice through the hand of the wisest man who ever lived (King Solomon), surely He Himself will follow His own advice. After all we are His children. Parents are told to punish their children for disobedience, not disown them, and it is the same way with God. God will not break the promise that He made to save your souls there is however another alternative if punishment doesn't correct the problem. If you continue in sin, even after God has disciplined you repeatedly, eventually God will not keep allowing you to be a negative representative in this world and He will take you out. In other words, eventually God will destroy your body, but your soul will still be saved. You may think the loving forgiving God that I believe in would never do that. You need to see things the way God does. Your physical life on the earth is only temporary, but your spiritual life is for eternity. Which one of these is more important in the long stretch? If God destroys the body to save the soul then He is doing this out of love. Not only for the sinner's soul, but for the souls that would be lost because of the evil influence or corrupted testimony. Therefore, I believe that the simple fact that the main reason we are left here on earth after we are saved is so we can represent God, then how would it look to mankind if God's own representatives could not be certain that they were saved. The verses below should make it clear that if anyone continues to sin after they are saved that eventually God will take them off the earth, but they will still be saved. If God was just going to take away their salvation, then what would be the purpose of rewards, or the loss of them? What would be the purpose of disciplining them? What would be the purpose of removing them from the earth? These are the things that our Father in heaven will do if a saved person doesn't live a life that is pleasing to God, He doesn't take away their son ship or their inheritance or their salvation. We may break our promises to God, but even if we do, God will not break His covenant with us. Another thing about God's point of view, yes God would be taking that person off the face of the earth, but they are going to heaven which we all know is a much better place. I don't believe anyone would regret that transition.

> *"If any man's work shall be burned, he shall suffer loss: but he himself shall be saved; yet so as by fire. Know ye not that ye are the temple of God, and that the Spirit of God dwelleth in you? If any man defile the temple of God, him shall God destroy; for the temple of God is holy, which temple ye are." (1Cor 3:15-17"*

> *"If his children forsake my law, and walk not in my judgments; If they break my statutes, and keep not my commandments; Then will I visit their transgression with the rod, and their iniquity with stripes. Nevertheless my loving kindness will I not utterly take from him, nor suffer my faithfulness to fail. My covenant will I not break, nor alter the thing that is gone out of my lips." (Ps 89:30-34)*

Chapter Twenty Seven

Purpose and Summary

The Purpose of this Book

The whole purpose of this book is to help those who are seeking God to find Him and to help those who have already found God to know absolutely for sure that they are saved and going to heaven and that their salvation cannot be taken from them regardless of what they do after they are saved. Before I close I would like to leave you with a brief summary of why this is true:

Personal Experiences

The first reason is because of my own personal experiences. Before I was saved I lived for the world and since I have been saved I have tried my best to live for God. I have not always done the right thing either before or after salvation, but God knows my heart and He knows that I am not the same person that I was before salvation. Before I was saved I knew there was something missing in my life. There was an emptiness that could not be filled, a desire that could not be satisfied, but since I have received the Holy Spirit in my life I have never felt that emptiness again. Before I was saved my life was motivated by self-satisfaction, since my redemption my desire is to please God and serve my fellowman. Before I was born again of the Spirit I wondered around in this world without direction allowing the Devil to use me in whatever way he chose, since I have been saved the voice of God inside me directs my paths and gives me direction and purpose. I am certain that I am saved because it changed everything about me.

I Understand God's Plan

I know that I am saved because now that I have received the Holy Spirit I now have understanding about God's plan for the world and especially for me. Before I was saved I had no desire to read God's Word and even if I did happen to read it I had no understanding. After I was saved I had a tremendous hunger for the Word of God and could never get enough of it. When you have the Holy Spirit He gives you spiritual guidance and helps you learn God's ways and understand the things that God says. He uses the Word of God to lead you on the path of righteousness.

I know that I am saved because of my desire to read, and my ability to understand God's Word and because of the desire that I have to live for God.

Everlasting Life

I am certain that I am going to heaven one day because God gave me everlasting life. Everlasting means without end and without interruption. If I could lose my salvation the term everlasting in God's description of Spiritual life would not be accurate because it would not be life without end. I cannot lose my salvation and get it back because if I could get it back I would have to crucify Christ again and put Him to open shame. God the Father would never allow that. The final sacrifice for sins has been made. If I could lose it and get it back then it would not be without interruption and therefore again the word "Everlasting" would not be an appropriate description of Spiritual life.

The Unpardonable Sin

I know for sure that I am saved and on my way to heaven because of the unpardonable sin. The only sin that Jesus said could never be forgiven is the blasphemy of the Holy Ghost. To blasphemy the Holy Ghost means to deny the power of God to indwell the believer with the Holy Spirit. Since it is the indwelling of the Holy Spirit that gives us eternal life, which happens when we accept Jesus Christ as our savior, then rejecting Christ as your savior is the same as blaspheming the Holy Spirit or denying that the Spirit of God has the power or authority to save.

A Free Gift from God

I have complete confidence in my salvation because salvation is not something that I deserve. Salvation is a free gift from God that is given only to those who trust in His Son Jesus. If salvation was something that I could earn by being a good person, then it would also be something that I could hold on to by continuing to be a good person. If it were possible for me to be a good enough person to get to heaven without a savior, then there would have been no reason for Jesus to come in the first place. It was God that saved me and it is God that keeps me saved.

Forgiven for Being a Sinner

I know I am saved because Jesus came to save sinners and I am qualified. I am just a saved sinner and I am no better than anyone else. I try to live righteously because I am a child of God and I want the world to witness and experience what God did for me. God doesn't forgive sins, He forgives sinners. Because I am a saved sinner when God looks down from heaven upon me He doesn't see all the sin that I have committed during my life time, He only sees the soul that has been cleansed by the sacrifice His Son Jesus made to save me. God forgave me for all the sins

I would ever commit in my lifetime, past, present and future. There is no sin that I can commit since I have been saved that has not already been forgiven from God's perspective.

Salvation is a Relationship

I know without a doubt that I am saved for all eternity because my salvation is based on a relationship not a fellowship. God created us and therefore He knew that He could not count on us to hold on to something so precious as our souls. He saved us and our salvation had to be based on something that we could not earn and it would not depend on us to keep it because if we could lose it we would. We can lose our fellowship with God by making simple sinful mistakes because in order to have fellowship with God you must be sinless. It is impossible for any human to remain sinless and so our salvation could not be maintained under such circumstances. That is why we are related to God through marriage. We are the Bride of His Son. I guess you could say that I am Gods daughter-in-law. Sounds funny, but I'll take a relationship with the heavenly Father any way I can get it. We are also related to God by birth, the spiritual birth that we received when we were born of the Spirit of God at the time that we accepted Christ. Finally, we are also, according to God's Word, related to Him by adoption. So we are related to God by marriage, by birth and by adoption. No matter what we do we cannot lose these relationships.

Kept by the Power of God

I am certain of my everlasting Spiritual life because my salvation is kept secured by the power of the Omnipotent (all powerful) God. I am not charged with the responsibility of keeping my salvation secure. It was not me that granted me salvation for myself, it was God that gave salvation to me and it is God that keeps it safe for me. Because of the fact that my salvation is not based on anything that I have done or ever will do, then it is safe and secure in the hands of God.

The Bride of Christ

My salvation is secure because I am the bride of Christ. Marriage is a God ordained institution that results in two separate people becoming one. This marriage relationship is a picture of what happens when a person gets saved and their spirit becomes one with the Spirit of God. It is this relationship with the Holy Spirit that makes us one with Christ and one with the Father. The Bible teaches that the husband is the head and the wife is the body. It also teaches that Jesus is the head of the church and the body of all born believers is the body of the church. Just as Jesus protects and guides the church so is the husband the guide and protector of the wife. God does not believe in divorce so even if man breaks his vows to his wife God will never do that to His church. The Bible says God hates divorce. (Mal 2:16) For more on this topic I would invite you all to read my book "God's Marriage and Man's Divorce".

No Condemnation

I know I am going to heaven because there is no condemnation to those that believe. Those who have been saved are never threatened with the loss of their salvation anywhere in God's Word. I find it difficult to believe that if it were possible for someone to lose such a precious gift as eternal life that it would be scattered all over God's Word with warning after warning that if you blow it, and lose your salvation, then there is no more hope for you. The Bible does tell us that if it were possible to lose it, it would be impossible to be saved again, but it never suggest that this could actually happen. This passage of scripture is a warning about false teachers and not about the seriousness of losing your salvation. There are no instructions anywhere in God's Word that tell anyone what to do if they lose their salvation because it is simply not possible.

A Gift from the Father

I am certain about my everlasting life because my salvation is a gift from God the Father to God the Son through the indwelling of God the Holy Spirit. God is a trichotomy, in other words, God consist of three separate parts. The Bible teaches that Christians are a gift from God the Father to His Son and this is accomplished by joining Christians to God by the indwelling of the Holy Spirit. I believe that since we are also created as a trichotomy and after the image of God, that God the Son Jesus is just as proud of the gifts that His Father gave Him as we are about the gifts that our fathers have given us. Jesus proclaims numerous times throughout the scriptures that we are gifts from His Father and that He will never lose anything that the Father left in His care and He will never cast it out.

Perfect Love Removes Fear

I believe salvation is eternal because God told us that His love inside us would eliminate fear. Truly, those who have never accepted God's plan for their salvation still have a lot of things to fear. Fear of He who can destroy both the body and soul in hell (God the Father) and fear of the wiles of the Devil. If I have been saved, then there is no more reason for me to fear God because He is my Father and He would never do anything to harm me. The only thing that I should fear is disobeying God and being disciplined for it. Discipline does not consist of the loss of my salvation because salvation is a relationship not a fellowship. I would no longer fear the Devil because God, who now lives in me, is greater than the Devil who is in control of this world. Perfect love casteth out fear. If I could lose my salvation, I would never be able to cast out fear. If for no other reason, I would always have the fear that I might do something that would cause me to lose it. I have no fear because I am saved and no-one can take that away. If I could lose my salvation, then fear could never be cast out.

Security Deposit

I am not concerned about losing my salvation because it is kept by the same power that gave it to me in the first place. My salvation is kept secure by the power of the Holy Spirit. The Holy Spirit is the down payment from God the Father on my inheritance that is waiting for me in heaven. The Holy Spirit is the earnest of our salvation. He is the security deposit on my eternal inheritance. He is the Spiritual life that lives inside of me which is God's guarantee that He will keep His promises to those who believe. The Holy Spirit that lives in me is my promise from God that I will be resurrected to eternal life with Him in heaven because it is the power of the Spirit that raised Jesus from the grave and it is the Spirit that lives in me that insures me of the same resurrection.

You Already Have Eternal Life

I am absolutely sure that my salvation is safe in God's hands because of the rapture. The Bible teaches us that there will come a day when Jesus will come back to retrieve those that He died for. It tells us that those who have died in Christ, or those who are asleep in Christ, will come up out of their graves first. After that, then those of us who are still alive when He comes will be changed and will go up into the clouds with those who rose from the grave and together we will ascend into heaven with Christ. The point is that our salvation is not caused by something that we do when Jesus comes to get us. Once we get saved, it doesn't matter what happens to us, even if we die, we are still saved and will still experience the resurrection. If you have accepted Christ as your savior then eternal life is not something you are still waiting for. If you have been saved, then you received eternal life at the moment you were indwelt with the Spirit of God. To be accurate we are still waiting for the transformation and glorification of our bodies, but we already have eternal life and nothing that happens after that can cause us to lose it, not even death.

Great Joy in Heaven

I know my salvation is safe in God's hands because there is great joy in heaven when someone gets saved. Since God is Omniscient (all knowing) He already knows ahead of time when someone will get saved and the entire heavenly host is waiting for this event to take place. There is great joy when someone is born into God's family through the indwelling of the Spirit just as there is when a new baby is born on earth. If it were possible for a person to lose their salvation, then there would be no reason to rejoice because God already knows ahead of time if that could happen also. Since it is not possible to lose it, then there is rejoicing because salvation is eternal like God is.

The Lamb of God

I know I am saved because Jesus is the Lamb of God that takes away the sins of the world, but more personably He is the Lamb of God that was sacrificed for my sins. In the Old Testament the Lamb was sacrificed to provide the blood that would cover the sins of the Israelites while the angel of the Lord passed over Egypt. The Israelites were passed over because their sins were hid from God the Father by the blood of the sacrificial lamb. God could no longer see their sins because they were covered by the blood. Today, if you are saved Jesus is the sacrificial lamb that was slain in order to cover your sins. When God looks down He does not see your sins He only sees the blood of the Lamb that was sacrificed to cover your sins. Once you are covered by the blood you are saved and that is the end of it.

Reservations in Heaven

My salvation is secured because I already have reservations in heaven. I have reservations that were made by God on my behalf. Jesus said He was going to prepare a place for us and He would be back to get us and take us home with Him. Not only has God made reservations for me in heaven, but He has already begun making preparations for my arrival. He is preparing a mansion for me in God's house and He is gathering the rewards that He will have waiting for me when I get there.

A Child of Promise

My everlasting life is a sure thing because I am a child of promise. In the Old Testament God made promises to Abraham because Abraham believed and trusted in God. The Bible says that Abraham believed God and it was counted unto him for righteousness. Abraham was justified by His faith in God the Father; this was the Old Testament, promise, or covenant between God and Abraham. The New Testament, or promise, or covenant of God is that anyone who would believe and trust in Jesus, His Son, their belief and trust would be counted unto them as righteousness. God went on to say, that even if they broke their promise to Him, that He would discipline them for their disobedience, but He would never break His promise to them of eternal life.

It is a Matter of Record

I know that I am safe and secure in the hands of God because my name has been written in the Lambs book of life. When you are born a natural birth your name is written in the book of life. When you are born the spiritual birth your name is written in the Lambs book of life. The Bible teaches that if your name is in the Lambs book of life that it will also remain in the book of life because you will live with God for eternity. If you are never born a Spiritual birth, then your name will be blotted out of the book of life as well because at the Great White Throne Judgment you will be cast into the Lake of fire where you will be separated from God for eternity. Your name cannot be blotted out of the Lambs book of life once it is entered in it because salvation cannot be taken away from you.

The Light of the World

I know my salvation is settled for eternity because God has given me the privilege and responsibility of being a light to the world. God is light and the world is full of darkness. Darkness represents the Devil and evil because it is the opposite of light. The reason that Christians are left here on the earth after they are born again is so that they can be a light in a dark world. My salvation is settled and if there wasn't a reason for God to leave me here I would be in heaven already, but He left me here because Jesus had to leave. While Jesus was here on the earth in the flesh He was the one who brought the light of God the Father to the world, but since Jesus had to go back to the Father He left us here to be the light. Christians are now the only means by which the gospel of Christ is spread to a lost world. If it were possible for me to lose my salvation, then I know I would lose it and so would millions of other Christians because it is impossible to live sinless. If I could lose my salvation I would not be a light to the world and Jesus would be ridiculed.

Predestination

I know that I am a forever born again child of God because of the doctrine of predestination. Whether you believe that predestination means that God has already predetermined that some will go to heaven and some will go to hell or not it really doesn't matter because what we do know for sure is that God is omniscient. He knows everything that has happened, everything that is happening and everything that will ever happen. Therefore it is obvious that God does know who will be saved and who will not be saved and He knows who will spend eternity in heaven and who will spend eternity in the lake of fire. I believe God knows this, but He does not influence man's destiny. Just because I know something is going to happen doesn't mean I caused it to happen. If there is rejoicing in heaven when a person is saved it can only be because they have been waiting for that person to be born of the Spirit. God already knew it was going to happen and so to Him your name being in the Lambs book of life is matter of fact that can't be changed. From God's perspective our future is His past.

Ambassadors for Christ

I believe that my salvation is everlasting because I have been appointed as an ambassador for Christ. I was left here on earth to represent Christ and the church (the body of Christ) and heaven and salvation. Everything that I was left here to represent is eternal as am I. If I could be Jesus' representative one day and be as lost as those that I am trying to reach for God the next day I would not be Christ's representative at all. Instead I would be a representative of Satan. It is Satan that wants people to believe that they can lose their salvation. If you can lose your salvation, then there is no point in obtaining it to begin with. Who would turn from being a sinner to serve God if in the end they are going to hell anyhow?

Led by the Spirit

I know that I am saved because I know I am led by the Holy Spirit of God. Before I had the Spirit in me I had no concern about the Bible or about the things of God or about other people. Now I know that the reason I was created was to please God. I know that if someone offends me that I should pray for them. I know that if someone takes my shoes I should offer them my socks. I know that I should not take anyone to court. I know that I should love my enemy and pray for God to forgive them. I know that the main reason that God blesses me with a good career is so that I will have to give to those in need. I know that no matter how much I give to help others that God will repay it because you can't out give God. I know that the reason I was left here on earth is to try to lead others to Christ. I know that I am a child of God because God gave me a new way of thinking and I know I am led by the Spirit of God that lives in me.

Born Again

I know that my eternal home will be in heaven because Jesus used the words "Born Again" to describe what happened to me when I accepted Christ. To be born again literally means to be conceived from above, to be the offspring of God, to be conceived by the Spirit of God. My second birth came from God through the work of the Holy Spirit. I was conceived of the Spirit of God just as Jesus was. It is the Spirit that will raise me from the dead at the resurrection the same as He raised Jesus from the dead. Jesus used the word "Born" because you can only be born one time naturally and you can only be born one time spiritually. You cannot be unborn naturally and you cannot be unborn spiritually. You cannot give your life back to your parents and you cannot give the Holy Spirit back to God. Your parents cannot take your life back from you and God cannot take His Spiritual life back from you either.

God Disciplines Me

I know that I am safe and secure in the hands of Jesus because God uses discipline to correct His children the same as my earthly father did. He does not take away my son ship. I have become a child of God the Father through the spiritual birth from the Holy Spirit. If God could take away my spiritual birth, my birthright, my inheritance, then why would He bother disciplining me? God disciplines me because He is my Father and no one can change that not even God Himself. You might say that God is all powerful and there is nothing that He cannot do, but you would be wrong. The one thing that God cannot do is break His own word, His own promises, or His own covenants. If God could take away my inheritance, then why would there be discipline and why would there be rewards? Even if God is so disappointed in my behavior that He feels that I must be removed from the earth because of my bad testimony, then He will destroy my body, but my soul will still go to heaven. If this is true, then it is obvious that no matter what I do, after that I have accepted Christ as my savior, that even though I might lose rewards, I might be disciplined, God might even destroy my body, but He will not and cannot take away my salvation.

My Desire for You

It is my sincere desire that, through the guidance of the Holy Spirit, I may have been helpful in shedding a little light on the plans that God has for you and your life. If you are reading this book, then chances are that God has already been working on you and you are looking for answers. God is drawing you to the light. I pray that whether you are searching for answers concerning your eternal destiny or trying to figure out what God wants you to do next, that you may have found some answers in these pages. If you have accepted Christ as your savior you no longer need to worry about the security of your salvation. You can now concentrate on developing and using the gifts that God has given you for God's glory. If these words have had an impact on your life or on your spirituality in any way I would like to hear about it. I would like to be able to thank and praise God for what He has done for you and pray for God to use you in a mighty way. Please send me an email with your story at Tinbender_dave@yahoo.com.

Your humble servant,
David Boudreaux

Printed in the USA
CPSIA information can be obtained
at www.ICGtesting.com
LVHW040029300124
770010LV00005B/6